The MAGIC of the REAL WORLD

KRISTINA WOOD

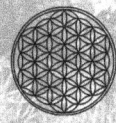
FLOWER of LIFE PRESS

 FLOWER *of* LIFE PRESS

Copyright © 2025 Kristina Wood

All rights reserved. No part of this book may be used or reproduced by any means, graphic, electronic, or mechanical, including photocopying, recording, taping, or by any information storage retrieval system without the written permission of the publisher except in the case of brief quotations embodied in critical articles and reviews.

Because of the dynamic nature of the Internet, any web addresses or links contained in this book may have changed since publication and may no longer be valid.

The views expressed in this work are solely those of the author and do not necessarily reflect the views of the publisher, and the publisher hereby disclaims any responsibility for them.

Published by Flower of Life Press
www.floweroflifepress.com
Jane Ashley, *Publisher*

Flower of Life Press books may be ordered through booksellers or by contacting: support@floweroflifepress.com

Cover and interior design by Jane Ashley

Library of Congress Control Number: Available upon request.

ISBN: 979-8-9987870-2-7

Dedication

This book is dedicated to my two children, who are now adults. When I called out for them to come and join us all here on Mother Earth, they slowly came like Lights from far out in the Universe. When they finally arrived, their Lights shone like lighthouses, reflecting brightly off the waters and showing people a safe passage. They are the most beautiful humans, full of love, sharing what we believe to be morally right and supporting other beings here on Earth with their hearts. I am so grateful for their presence in my life. This book tells the amazing stories about how they came to be here with us.

"'Split a piece of wood; I am there. Lift up the stone, and you'll find me there,' says Yeshua in the Gospel of Thomas. Open Kristina Wood's book of wonder, and you'll find a way back to your Source there."

~Lars Muhl, *Danish Mystic, Film Producer,*
Author of The O Manuscript

"I worked with Kristina on some of the sections of this book in an earlier form, so I know the time and diligence she has put into it. I also know Kristina to be a deeply kind and generous soul. Her offering this work to the world now comes from her sincere and lifelong commitment to live in gratitude and with beauty. Her own remarkable story makes a powerful foundation for presenting these evolving truths. I have taken her Mystical Journeys course and found it thrilling and yet very accessible. It feels as if Kristina's whole wish is to encourage and enliven people to live in deeper, truer contact with the natural world—to the beauty, majesty, and wisdom that is available to us all—if we choose to look and listen. I cast wild blessing over the whole project from my heart, which has been opened again and again by my association with Kristina."

~Jenny D'Angelo, *Author of* Connect with Your Angels:
A Guide for Everyone *and a new chapbook,* Saved

"Kristina not only urges us to have a more enchanted relationship with the natural world, she offers a proven path and practices to help open the doorways of perception to magic, connection, and beauty."

~Stephen Dinan, *Founder of Shift Network*

"This beautifully written book brings to our awareness the incredible real world we live in, with all its magic and miracles. At a time when we are searching for who we really are, it connects us with who Mother Earth really is. The meditations are wonderful, the words seemed to jump right off the page into my heart. This is a delightfully powerful read!"

~*Trudy Woodcock, Founder of Maya Wisdom Circle*

"The Magic of the Real World *is a beautifully written spiritual book that provides a path for seekers to learn to observe the wonders of the everyday world and recognize the deep messages and profound significance woven into the fabric of daily existence. Through radiant meditations that capture the essence of sight, sound, and touch, the reader can learn to attune to the rhythms of the Earth and find the unconditional love that unlocks the magic of the secret world beyond. Let this book be your guide to finding the sacred in the simplest moments and awaken to the extraordinary magic that is always present just beneath the surface of daily life.*"

~*Mary Ann Keatley, Ph.D., Author and Artist*

"Reading The Magic of the Real World *feels like stepping into a sacred circle of Earth's wisdom keepers. Kristina Wood's words carry the heartbeat of Mother Earth, the laughter of dolphins, and the whispers of trees. Each story and meditation is a doorway into greater love, healing, and awakening; a gift of beauty and light for anyone seeking to remember their place in the living web of creation.*"

~*Kathy Mason, Conscious Business Alchemist, Author, AI Consultant, and Podcast Host of Conscious Business Zone*

"Kristina Wood offers us a profound healing vision for humanity and sacred Nature in this powerful and visually gorgeous book. The Magic of the Real World draws on her own remarkable transcendent experiences in some of the world's most deeply sacred and beautiful places. Peopled with a cast of undeniably real nature spirits, angelic beings, and spirit guides of great wisdom, the book takes us on an enthralling journey of the soul, from the mystic dolphins of the far Pacific to the spiritually rarified heights of Mt. Shasta, with precious teachings shared along the way which show us the wondrous paths and transformative practices so desperately needed at this pivotal time. Truly, a book for this year and all years, to bring us home to Nature and home to our souls."

~Michael Henry Dunn, Author of Romancing the Divine, Musician, Actor, Sacred Activist and Founding Director of the Sacred Academy of Geo-Energetics

"The Magic of the Real World is a luminous, inspiring collection of mystical stories and meditations. Kristina Wood invites us into realms of wonder and healing while reminding us that these gifts are not hers alone—they belong to all of us. Her stories pave a path for each of us to awaken our own mystical gifts and live in deeper communion with the sacred dimensions of life. Reading this book feels like being guided through a series of doorways into the unseen world. Each tale carries both beauty and practical wisdom, reminding us of our sacred connection with Earth and cosmos. It is a heartfelt offering of hope, vision, and empowerment for these times."

~Devaa Haley Mitchell, Co-Founder, The Shift Network

Contents

Foreword by Andrew Harvey xi
Introduction 1
    The Real World That Surrounds Us 5
    Finding the Magic in My Own Life 11
    Travels in Mt. Shasta 29
    Spirals and Chakras Meditation 41
    Sunrise 49
    Search for Panther Springs 51
    St. Germaine and the Violet Flame Meditation 64
    Deer People 71
    Dolphin Journey 73
    Meditation for Healing in Our Ocean Waters 83
    Our Water 89
    The Fairie Hill 91
    Meditation with Mother Earth 98
    Dancing Trees, Transfiguring 105
    In Balance with Sekhmet 107
    Meditation with Sekhmet 114
    Fire Lover 121
    What is Abu Ghurab? 123
    Meditation with the Pleiades 133
    River Messages 141
    Selva and the First Prophets 143
    Meditation with the Tree of Life 158
    Super Full Moon 163
    Conclusion 171
    The Prayer of St. Francis 181
Acknowledgments 183
About the Author 185

FOREWORD

By Andrew Harvey

In these wild, chaotic, infinitely dangerous times, when humanity is on the edge of destroying itself through annihilating its environment, nothing is more important for all of us than to wake up to the creation as a manifestation of the divine consciousness we are all secretly one with.

The common testimony of all the great mystical traditions is that there is one reality with multiple levels of emanation, all of which are secretly crystallized light. What this means is that we live as holograms of the One in a universe that is fundamentally created from a love and joy that we can connect with only if we develop through sacred practice the eyes, ears, and hands with which to celebrate.

Kristina Wood has written a wonderful, vibrant, unique and completely original book in which she unveils her own hilarious and ecstatic experiences with one of the realms of the One that we normally in our culture have very little connection with but which is waiting to befriend, enchant, and infuse us with wonder and the strength to rise up and claim our human divine identity and remake the world.

Many years ago, I was sitting with an Aboriginal elder near Ayers Rock on a rusty tin barrel. Suddenly he asked me, "Would you like to see the tree spirits?" I said I would be delighted. He taught me a simple exercise and made me look at a group of bedraggled desert trees for an hour. Nothing whatever happened and I came back humbled and disappointed.

He burst out laughing, clapped his hands, and said, "I knew it wouldn't be easy for you. You're too stuck in your mystical mind, but I have asked the tree spirits to reveal themselves, and I promise you, they will."

Later that afternoon, I went to a funky abandoned motel full of rowdy cowboys and weird-looking recluses with long mustaches, where I was staying. I sat out on a tin chair and gazed at the tree in the courtyard, and

The Magic of the Real World

suddenly, to my absolute delight and amazement, I saw a tangle of tree spirits that were irrepressibly funny and playful, embracing and dancing up and down the trunk and along the branches. They were staring at me, pointing at me and giggling as our glances met. And their total fluid joy filled me with rapture. I have never seen them again, but now I know that wherever I am, where trees are, they are there. And I often bow my head to them and smile.

This experience opened me to the world of elves, spirits, gnomes and apparitions of every conceivable kind (and some inconceivable) that actually surround us and are longing to get in contact with us, so we can be awakened to and emboldened by the wildly magical nature of authentic reality and find the will and strength to do everything we can to preserve the extraordinary theater we are playing our human roles in.

Far too often, modern seekers pursue only the transcendent light and forget that that light, out of its own fabulous creative power, has taken form in millions of different worlds and realms of existence. We are the children both of the absolute godhead and the embodied godhead, and because of our essential divine childhood and divine grace, we have access to so many more sources of delight, awe, and amazement than a reductionist scientific philosophy that claims to know what the real world is but could never begin to imagine it.

Kristina Wood has a fine, precise, honed mind and a great gift of clarity, but instead of putting these gifts in the service of a constricted and sterile vision, she has dedicated them fearlessly, because of her own extraordinary experience, to the celebration of one multifaceted, foaming, exuberant mind and heart-dazzling aspect of the reality we all now desperately need to wake up to, before we ruin in our self-created depressed ignorance, our fabulous world.

I salute Kristina for her courage, her wild, unfettered spirit, and her passion to communicate to us what has been communicated to her. I encourage seekers on all paths to read and learn from *The Magic of the Real World* and to start opening to the outrageous and transformative possibilities that it so generously opens for us.

I also salute her for the truly wonderful practices written with such gorgeous enthusiasm that she peppers her text with. I have done them myself, experienced their expansiveness and find them completely aligned with the vision of the birth of a new divine humanity that is at the core of my work. I am so grateful to Kristina for her pioneering *chutzpah*. The tree spirits I saw in Australia are all celebrating the coming out of the little people in this amazing work.

Dare to celebrate with them.

Andrew Harvey
Oak Park Illinois
February, 2025

Introduction

This book is my prayer for humanity at this time, when our survival and the survival of a great part of Nature are threatened. My intention is to establish a wholly new, although profoundly ancient, relationship with Creation, one that requires three kinds of inspiration to be born in all of us.

1. To realize that we are the children of the Earth—all of us, from the tiniest flea to the majestic, leaping whale.
2. The inspiration to allow ourselves to be filled with the ecstasy and the empowered truth of this amazing reality.
3. The inspiration to act calmly but urgently at all levels for our human world to protect our Mother, the Earth: her endangered seas, fields, animals, and so, ourselves.

My adventure into the wonderful world I shall present to you began with 30 years of ceremonial experiences with the Lakota People. Their passionate dedication to Mother Earth and its precise wonder, together with their age-long, mature skillfulness, rich reverence, ecstatic joy, radical humility, and all-inclusive awe, have miraculously not been completely lost, despite the sordid and brutal attempts by the patriarchal religions and militaries of my own ancestors. Those violent attempts to annihilate an entire way of life that they could not understand did not completely prevail. However, my own indigenous connection with the Divine Mother in Nature had been lost. The generous Lakota revealed their spirituality to me in stages over three decades. I see now how much I desperately needed their teachings.

All of us yearn to have undeniable experiences with the Divine. The Lakotas taught me that this cannot be for private ecstasy. We must surrender to receive the truth of what the cosmos is offering us; to receive its extravagant blessing and put the joy and empowerment this gives us into wise action to defend the glory of what is, against all the forces in our modern world that are clearly threatening its destruction.

We must now abandon purely abstract dogmas and come into a vibrant relationship with all of life so that we can evolve practices that urgently deepen our communion with creation and give us the inspiration and strength to come together to save our planet and humanity. For example, when we simply see the Morning Star, we can sing a song, say a prayer, and ask for a Good Day.

We are all indigenous to Mother Earth. Our Mother Earth is our source, our blood, our bones. Everything we are is made from her. We are each, in the depths of our whole beings, her children. This is a visceral relationship; we come from her belly.

We are now being asked to retrieve ancient spiritual technologies that open our hearts and minds to become naked and intimate with the sacred. Our next responsibility as the human race is to relearn about our indigenous connection with Mother Earth, and this can come in many ways. To begin with, it is essential to realize that our true wealth lies in our awakened consciousness and the transformed and gorgeous perceptions that arise from it.

We must be awake to what is happening all around us. We are all connected to everything in the Universe because it is all connected to us. Through the power of our awakened perception, we can truly and magically transform our lives. It means entering into the Creation as a dazzlingly interconnected field of love where we find self-regenerating joy. Intimacy with nature is the revelation that opens to us our true beauty and power. All things are singing the truth of the spirit. Living things, the birds, the trees, the stones, welcome you. All of creation knows that you are blessed already and are loved exactly the way you are. Everything in nature is longing to give you everything you need to live the fullest life imaginable.

We cannot waste any more time refusing to let in this astounding and all-transforming love. We are loved by so many beings here on Earth…as we are kissed by the flowers, moved by the moon, swayed by the waves, ignited by the fires. We have to now receive this love and repay it in respect and sacred action.

Introduction

Despite our appalling treatment of her, the Mother still remains unbelievably loving towards us. We have no time now *not* to experience this love, but to recognize the fantasies of separation that have made us so lonely and destructive and start, empowered by that Mother Love, to come together to save ourselves and our Earth.

From *Calling the Spirit Back from Wandering the Earth in Its Human Feet*[1]

> *When you find your way to the circle, to the fire kept burning by the keepers of your soul, you will be welcomed.*
>
> *You must clean yourself with cedar, sage, or other healing plant.*
>
> *Cut the ties you have to failure and shame.*
>
> *Let go the pain you are holding in your mind, your shoulders, your heart, all the way to your feet. Let go the pain of your ancestors to make way for those who are heading in our direction.*
>
> *Ask for forgiveness.*
>
> *Call upon the help of those who love you. These helpers take many forms: animal, element, bird, angel, saint, stone, or ancestor.*
>
> *Call your spirit back. It may be caught in corners and creases of shame, judgment, and human abuse.*
>
> *You must call in a way that your spirit will want to return.*
>
> *Speak to it as you would to a beloved child.*
>
> *Welcome your spirit back from its wandering. It may return in pieces, in tatters. Gather them together. They will be happy to be found after being lost for so long.*

---

1 Reprinted from *Conflict Resolution for Holy Beings* by Joy Harjo. Copyright © 2015 by Joy Harjo. Used with permission of the publisher, W. W. Norton & Company, Inc. All rights reserved.

The Real World That Surrounds Us

I do apologize for the disturbing nature of information found in these first paragraphs. However, it is the reality of our world today. We must review the scope of our alarming times, simply to keep it all in mind as we look at options for how we can understand the Magic of the Real World we live in.

It is safe to say that we have been in denial regarding the sacredness of our Earth and all the goodness of the Beings that exist here with us. Below, I list just some of the effects from the disrespect we have shown and the consequences that we are facing today.

- Children are being murdered, even decapitated, because of AR-15 war weapons in their schools, churches, parks, even their homes. Over five million children are sex trafficked every year.
- Apocalyptic wildfires rage across the globe, sometimes hundreds of them in the course of one day, every summer.
- 47% of mammals, 23% of birds are dying because of the effects of climate change.
- Out-of-control floods are causing loss of every type of animal life (including human), countless homes, expensive infrastructure, as well as erosion and economic disaster.
- We are running out of fresh drinking water and soon out of food supplies; seven billion people need fossil fuels just to cook; air pollution causes seven million deaths per year.
- The great Pacific Garbage Patch spans 1.6 million sq. kilometers, starving fish and destroying reefs. It is now too late to save the Arctic summer Ice. The waters close to our southern beaches are so warm, they are destroying the coral reefs.

- Our liberties are being stripped away: In Uganda, you will be put to death for loving whomever you please. In some states in America, you cannot read the books that you want, love the people you want, or control your own health.
- There are wars in Europe, Africa, South America, the Middle East; Russia is threatening a complete nuclear world disaster.
- Artificial Intelligence could create an ever-powerful authority without morals that could rob us of our autonomy and even destroy our world.

We, the inhabitants of Earth, have created all this havoc and destruction, yet despite these horrific realities, we have a beautiful world full of loving spirits, so how has this tragedy happened? It seems that we humans think it is all about us and how much money we want and how many things we need, yet we have an amazing Earth that wants to offer us so much love.

I want to share with you about the real world that surrounds us on our beautiful Earth, to assure you that there are many Beings here who really care about us. They have been here forever and helped to support our Earth with an interdependent intelligence throughout time.

The Earth is actually teeming with life beyond what is apparent. There is an entire web vibrating with energy that may have helped preserve us so far. That includes the ones we know and see—animals, plants and trees—as well as unseen beings like Angels, Elves, Fairies, Gnomes and many different Light Beings.

With all the extreme changes affecting our Earth now, we each need to expand our awareness to connect with the central wisdom that is held by our Earth—also called Gaia—and all her participants. We have an important purpose to realize the existence of these energies and create relevant stories with them. If we can connect with them, they will help us in thrilling and astonishing ways. Learning to communicate with the larger eco-field is an important new frontier for humanity.

- Many of us are upset about the challenges surrounding our creation and want to help the world to overcome its seemingly insurmountable problems. But as one Tibetan monk suggested, we can't simply be angry people screaming for peace. We need to work on two levels: we do need to contribute to social activism but perhaps more importantly, we need personal healing. One way to heal ourselves is with truthful stories that remind us of our indebtedness to the creation that we inhabit.
- Shamanism provides a spiritual process that anyone interested in personal healing can follow because it is a human path. It helps us connect our hearts to the Earth, like the roots of a tree. It allows us to see and hear magical stories of journeys into important new interconnected realities. Shamanism is not simply about seeing auras and witnessing miracles; it is about cultivating a mode of perception in which everyday life is animated with beauty, wonder and meaning. It is about awakening our spirits and cultivating awareness that we are connected to everything in the universe. Through that power of perception, we can transform our lives. Visualizing these new myths may even help us save ourselves and heal our planet.

The shamanic visions related in this book are like modern fairy tales, a kind of dazzling and enchanted wisdom from Nature that helps us escape the prolific dis-ease that abounds on Earth.

At the end of each of the seven stories that follow, I present a rich, precise, and transformative meditation to help you develop the capacity to attune to these realms and go deeper into the healing experience. To help you enter into the radiance of the experience, I recorded these meditations with music and provide links with a QR code. I hope that you enjoy them.

Each meditation represents a journey that can guide us into recovering a clear view of our position in the Universe as well as conveying how we might help ourselves and others. We each have extraordinary powers within us: to love, see, hear, know, and bless, and they are just waiting to be developed.

Meditations are important because they allow us to escape the chaos of our world as we look for the truth within ourselves. The best way to understand the outside world is to go within so that we can learn to trust and believe in ourselves.

I did not plan to write these stories until my mentor, the author and mystic Andrew Harvey, suggested that I do so. He helped me understand that it is essential at this time in our world that we share whatever we can that might benefit us all. Many are in pain, but there is a tremendous, secret world awaiting us right here on Earth. This is the symbolic world, and it can initiate us into a new sense of peace and compassion.

As a result, this book is filled with the memories of my experiences in other dimensions, places where I found amazing insights into life. The visualizations related herein were healing and meaningful experiences for me. These beautiful visions, seen right here on Earth, gave me a new understanding and hope about many wonderful concepts. I share these stories as my humble offering to you. It is my deepest wish that you will find value in reading them and that they will inspire you to experience the wisdom, encouragement, and persistent creative energy that they ignite.

We are interdimensional beings who come from the stars. This is what I have been taught by my elders and my friends, the medicine people. If you also believe we are these beings, you will resonate with this book. It is written from the world of dreams and imagination, crossing the threshold of what is known and what is unknown. In the stories, I share vivid experiences from my time in the fifth dimension, a place that yields absolute freedom and liberation from human protocols; It is where we can access the codes of our future potential.

We are each a part of this cosmic wisdom. Our power to imagine is our cosmic connection for transformation. In our world today with its many challenges, it is important to be ready and available for any opportunity involving transformative action.

We are learning to recognize these openings as critical opportunities when they come along. This transformative capability is needed now as we strive for healing on many levels.

The experiences in these stories could be categorized as shamanic. Shamanic journeying gives access to higher guidance from spirit allies in other realms who help us navigate our lives with more wisdom and clarity. Shamans throughout the ages have been artists, poets, and visionaries because of their capacity to speak metaphorically and through imagery.

With that in mind, I also included some poems sandwiched appropriately into this collection from the fifth dimension. Each of the seven visionary stories is followed by a section called "Pondering Notes." These consist of the important reflections with which I have spent a considerable amount of time—even years—to make more sense of the visions.

During the 30 years that I spent time in ceremony with my Lakota friends, I never expected my experiences with these beautiful people to result in shamanic visions. However, those years primed me for some astonishing realizations that completely changed my life.

Finding the Magic in My Own Life

I have lived a very privileged life because of some special teachers whom I was gifted to be with and learn from. I want to share a few stories about my experiences with them. I was 33 years old, married, and having enough sex that I should have been pregnant, after five years of trying, but I wasn't, so I went to a special gynecologist down in the big city to find out what the problem was and had some tests done.

The results indicated that I had been born with some deformity in my reproductive system. I had only half a uterus and one of my fallopian tubes was clearly not attached to the missing part. The other tube was completely blocked. They told me that the only possible solution for a successful pregnancy would be major surgery. The doctors would take my good fallopian tube and attach it to the part of my uterus that was there. Then they would remove the old blocked one. I immediately knew, "No! Not that." I believed there had to be a better way.

The diagnosis provoked a huge reaction in me. This was not fair! Where was my future of being a mother with the joy of having wonderful children? Had these future dreams all died? I wanted the great gift of being able to create life. Driving home, I cried all the way, two hours up into the mountains of Colorado.

I had asked the doctor if I could adopt a baby. He offered no hope. "That is almost impossible these days." I was devastated. I felt annihilated. Like most girls born in the 1950s, I grew up with the clear expectation that my life included being a mom. I wanted to have kids to share my life and to have fun with. I felt that was part of my purpose. And now the doctors were telling me that it was not going to be. It felt like hell! How could this death happen to me with so many years of life left? It was beyond the dark night of the soul. I felt completely devastated and spent many weeks in tears.

After a few months in deep sadness, I decided to work to heal myself. I would be willing to surrender to God's will, but would persist with the strong intention to become a birther of new life, a person in charge of my own destiny.

These were back in the days of tape decks, so I bought some healing tapes in December and started listening to them. It was my New Year's resolution to fix the situation.

At the time, I was coaching swimmers in the small ski town of Frisco. We had a good little team because frankly, I was a great coach. I had competed in the 1968 Olympic Games in Mexico City and I knew a lot about swimming. I was also studying Jean Houston's teachings, regarding her exciting new revelations about the Human Potential Movement. I was relating all this wisdom to my swimmers. They were very successful. A few on my little team were in the top ten in the USA. They trained hard every morning before school and in the afternoons as well.

After the morning workouts, I'd go home, turn on my healing tape, and listen for an hour. It was a perfect program for me because I was wide awake after coaching for an hour and a half, starting at 5:00 in the morning. My husband had already left for work when I'd settle into the pillows on the balcony. There, I was able to focus on the healing messages.

I asked for healing. I asked for new life. I prayed to become a mother, somehow. Any possible way was alright with me. Amazingly, I kept up this practice for over eight months, doing it just about every morning. Suddenly, in the middle of August as I was listening to my healing prayer tapes, I observed an amazing thing. Up in the clouds through the skylight, I saw an absolutely beautiful girl in a chariot pulled by horses. She had long brown hair that was blowing in the wind. She smiled down at me as she flew by, waving happily. Then she said the most surprising words. "My name is Anna and I will be coming to be with you soon." Wow!

I told my husband about this. He thought it was interesting, but he was not entirely convinced until a friend of his, with whom he had talked about adopting children, called him a week later. He said, "We have a friend whose relative would like to give her child up for adoption. The girl is only sixteen, and she thinks her baby would have a better life with adoptive parents." Yes! We were interested. The baby was to be born in a few weeks. The very next weekend, my parents were coming for a visit over the Labor Day holiday.

After they arrived, we got the call. The baby would be born that weekend, instead of in a few weeks. She was born on September 1, precisely nine months after I started my healing sessions on the balcony. After some great negotiations by my husband, the local judges authorized the adoption. We went to the hospital, so excited. We took her home with us the very next day.

Of course, her name was Anna. It was so great to have my folks there because we had no idea how to feed, bathe, dress, or even change diapers for this beautiful baby girl. My mom, who had had four children and was a nurse, helped with everything. It was really fun. Anna slept in a cozy drawer until we could get out and buy a rocking cradle for our sweet doll baby. Life was everything I had hoped for with my new baby. I was especially happy. I quit my job as a swim coach so I could be with her as much as possible.

During the next few years, I had time to do other things since I was no longer coaching. I was invited to a Women's Circle in Crestone, Colorado, where I met an amazing Lakota spiritual guide named Irma Bear Stops. She was so much fun and we connected right away. We stayed in touch after that first meeting and I talked with her often. She came to visit me in Colorado and I was invited to her home in South Dakota on the Pine Ridge Reservation. When there, I came to appreciate the hunger and suffering that her people were experiencing. I began to organize sending Christmas presents for the children, coats for the elders, and money for heating their homes.

I had developed a prosperous business during the years after coaching. So, when Irma started calling once or twice a month asking for donations for her tribe, I was happy to give them. Once she needed funds to buy a lawn mower for the Sundance grounds; another time, funds for chainsaws to cut wood for sweat lodges. I was so happy to support her and her community. She invited me up to the Sundance, which was a newly emerging ceremony on the reservation, previously suppressed there under the U.S. government.

I began attending these ceremonies and Irma started teaching me. She taught me about the wind and how it was possible to actually hear messages and understand what is going on by simply feeling the direction of the wind. Reading the clouds was another lesson that I learned from her. She taught me about many of the indigenous medicine plants and how to harvest them for healing, and all the protocols of attending the Sundance as a supporter. I especially remember attending one Sundance in a long, rather see-through skirt, which I chose to wear because of the heat. She definitely set me straight on that. It was not proper to wear anything see-through in front of Lakota warriors who were Sundancing, or actually, ever in front of men on the reservation. This was not a proper thing for white women (or actually, any women) to do. Although it was sometimes embarrassing, I truly appreciated her teachings.

I loved being with her because she was so much fun, always joking, with a beautiful attitude toward life. She pointed out to me the eagles, yellow birds, and coyotes, explaining the power of each animal. Also, she was strong. I always felt safe and protected around her. Everything would be all right if I was in her presence. One time, I was at her humble home when a tornado was threatening. She taught me how to take the sacred pipe and hold it with the stem of the pipe pointing toward the danger. Then, to strongly tell the storm to go away. And it did.

She had had cancer since her early twenties, but everyone knew that the spirits were keeping her alive. She smoked like a chimney and was overweight. None of this phased her. She kept the order in her little town, bossing people around and telling them what was unacceptable behavior. She helped everyone and that truly was her reason for living. She lived her life as the strong medicine woman that she was, singing her sacred Lakota songs as powerfully as any man. I asked her if she was a medicine woman, but she consistently denied it.

I remember one time when I was up there for a ceremony and had to cook the meal, but she was out of gas for her stove. Since it was Sunday, we could not get any gas. She told me just to go ahead and cook anyway, so I did. I guess she simply manifested the gas, because there was just enough fuel to finish cooking, and the meal was perfect.

She was in her early sixties when we were in Colorado with the snow blowing, loading a truck full of furniture, coats, and more Christmas gifts. Our plan was to drive seven hours in the winter driving conditions from Colorado, up through the Nebraska sandhills and the South Dakota plains to her hometown on the Pine Ridge Indian Reservation. The truck was already overloaded, but there were still some things lying on the ground. She insisted that we take them all. She climbed on top of the huge pile, put everything that remained up there, securing it all with ropes, tying everything tightly.

I was amazed that she would not leave anything behind that could benefit her community. More than that, I could hardly believe that she would climb up on top of the overloaded truck in the snow and insist on tying it all down. She did it perfectly, and we made it up to the reservation intact.

As the needs in her community increased, Irma did not hesitate to ask me for contributions, and I was always happy to help. I talked with her almost every day. She was a great friend whom I admired immensely. One day, I got another call, this time asking for the money to get her favorite son, living in Oklahoma, up to the Sundance in South Dakota. The bus ticket was only $80. Of course, I would do that.

Then she asked the question that I had long been anticipating. "What would you like to have more than anything?" I immediately knew the answer. "I would like another child!" Without knowing any of the physical challenges around that issue, she said, just like a fairy godmother, "That you shall have!" She believed anything was possible. "You must come up to the community for a special ceremony with the Medicine Man."

We planned the trip, my husband, Anna, and I. It was in December when we arrived up on the Pine Ridge Reservation and we found a very tough, cold, and desolate environment. We had packed most things we needed for the ceremony: food to cook the ceremony meal, bottled water, even toilet paper. We also brought extra fruit, a rare commodity up there in those days, and lots of meat for them to live on for a while. Most importantly, we brought the sacred tobacco and fabric with which to construct tobacco prayer ties.

Immediately upon arrival, we got to work preparing for the ceremony. First, we had to track down the Medicine Man and present the pipe to him, asking for the privilege and favor of the ceremony. Of course, Irma showed me how to prepare the pipe and explained exactly what to do. I put my prayers into this pipe. The Medicine Man was a relative of Irma's. She had watched him grow up and at a very young age, he was able to talk with the clouds and stop the rain, if needed. He came from a lineage of powerful medicine men and his great, great grandfather had been the Medicine Man for Crazy Horse. He had orchestrated the ability for Crazy Horse to repel bullets with his own body as he rode through battles. We were working with one of the most respected, humble, and powerful medicine men left on the reservation.

There are many things required for a proper ceremony. Irma sent her younger son out to cut the sacred choke cherry sticks that we needed. I started making the tobacco prayer ties, 75 of them for this particular ceremony. Then we needed to cook beef stew, potato salad (a favorite of Irma's), *wojape*, a traditional Lakota berry soup. We also had to bake the cake, organize the crackers and bread, and make some coffee. When the choke cherry sticks came back to the house, we prepared them for ceremony by cutting them to the proper length, skinning them of their bark, and tying special tobacco offerings on them. It was a bunch of work and a happy time. Anna played with Irma's grandchildren who lived next door. Finally, everything was ready. We covered all the pots of food with aluminum foil and tied the tops on with strings, gathered up serving utensils, put the sacred sticks and tobacco ties into plastic bags, and loaded it all into the back of the pickup. Away we went into the country in the cold, dark night to the ceremony house.

We did not want to be late, so we sat there waiting in the truck under the brilliant stars of the black night skies above the South Dakota prairie. In time, people started to arrive. Finally, someone came and unlocked the ceremony house which consisted of a small room, windows covered with blankets, and drums hanging on the walls—all ancient, special ceremonial relics. In the corner were paper plates, bowls, and plastic utensils for serving the ceremony food. We placed all the food in the middle of the room on the floor.

At about 11:00 p.m., the Medicine Man arrived with his parents. He carried his father up the stairs and into the room. His parents were an integral part of the ceremony because they symbolized the ultimate support; they sang the songs and started both the pipe round and the water round. They were there adding power to the ceremony and making sure everything was done correctly, even though the Medicine Man knew exactly how to do it. The singers had their drum and the door was locked. We were set to start.

All the lights went out, and in the dark, the drumming started. The ancient Lakota ceremony songs began pounding in our ears. We sat there in amazement as we heard the stomping of animal spirits on the floor and watched sparks of light ignite all around the altar that had been carefully set up. An entire series of songs continued, honoring the Four Directions, prayers for healing, and for thanks. Then it was my turn to pray for what I wanted. I prayed that I could please have a healthy child from my own body.

More prayer songs, more thanksgiving songs. Then, finally the beautiful ceremony was over. On came the lights. The sacred pipe was sent around the circle of the room where everyone had gathered for the ceremony. We each had a smoke connecting us to the spirits, the prayers. Next, the sacred water was passed around by one of the helpers. Everyone was respectfully still in deep prayer. After that, the silence was broken and the paper plates handed out. Two helpers served the food. We laughed at the jokes the Medicine Man and others told while we ate the sacred medicine food. It was now about 1:00 a.m.

After it was over, I asked Irma what the message from the spirits was, because it had been delivered in Lakota. She told me they said this problem was not my fault, that they would help me, but I would need to drink a special tea made of herbs from the land that was being prepared for me. I was to drink it for four days and stay away from all people for another four days. Before I left Irma's house, she told me to ask the Medicine Man's mother to make a star quilt for my new baby. In Lakota culture when you are wrapped in a star quilt, your ancestors are surrounding you in a helpful way, so I agreed to do that. I started drinking the tea and we left for Colorado.

The months passed: January, February, March, April, May, June, July. I waited patiently. In August, I received an urgent call from Irma. She had been at the home of the Medicine Man's mother and inquired about the star quilt for my baby. But she was told, "It will not be made because that baby will not be born!"

But Irma was undeterred, telling me on the phone, "You WILL have your baby. For this to happen, you must come up here for four nights of sacred Yuwipi ceremonies." She sounded so sure about it, I began to make plans right away to go up there.

My husband decided that he would not go, because it would be at least a week away from work, so I packed up the truck with all the needed supplies and Anna and off we went.

When I got there, Irma told me that the most important thing for me to do was to learn how to pray so that my dream would come true. This is what Irma taught me for the next week, every hour, every day. It was like arriving at the University of Life and only having one week to learn the lessons of a lifetime.

She taught me how to tie 405 tobacco prayer ties, create the flags to honor the Four Directions, prepare the choke cherry sticks with tobacco ties, cook the offering dinner, and get the ceremonial water. I was to do all this every day for four days. But the most important thing she taught me was how to fill the pipe with prayers. She explained that the only way these prayers could be fulfilled would be if I completely believed in the desired outcome. She cited examples, including herself, of people on the reservation who should have died long ago, but because of prayers filled with the belief in the goodness and mercy of Tunkashila, the Creator, these folks were still alive.

I listened to Irma. I tried hard to do everything she told me to do. It was intense. Sometimes I stepped in front of sacred items, which was considered very irreverent. She was not patient with me. Learning to pray with complete conviction and faith that these prayers would be heard entailed so much concentration. I was exhausted. We got up early every day to get everything done. Driving through the dark countryside, we often did not get home from the ceremonies until 2:00 or 3:00 a.m. This was a test. How much did I want it?

The Yuwipi ceremony is a special, powerful ceremony. The Medicine Man gets wrapped up with ropes in tight knots. His hands are tied behind his back, feet together, and he is laid face down on the floor on a buffalo skin with sage. After smudging, the lights go out and the drummers sing their beautiful Lakota songs with the community joining in. The spirit lights start flashing around the darkened room, animal spirits are heard stomping on the floor. It feels powerful. The most special part for me was feeling the tiny, spirit hands doctoring me. They would pat me all over my abdomen, chest, and my head. The loving touch was the most tender, special thing that has ever happened to me in ceremony. At the end, the lights come on and there is the Medicine Man sitting up on his buffalo skin, miraculously unwrapped from his ropes and ready to give the messages from the spirits. They had been delivered to him in a special language that only trained medicine men can understand.

All four nights, I prayed for a son (since I already had a beautiful daughter), for a child who would be strong, kind, healthy, and wise. Every night, Irma told me what the Medicine Man's message was: that I was praying with a lot of faith. As I witnessed all this intense prayer by the medicine people and the community for me and the other people who were being doctored for various health problems, I completely believed in what I was doing. Irma continued to instruct me in having strong faith in my prayers, and with those magical little spirit hands doctoring me, my amazement and belief grew. On the fourth night of these ceremonies, the Medicine Man had a message for me: You must come back in one year for a thanksgiving ceremony celebrating your baby boy. Then we will give him his Lakota name.

Six weeks later, I was pregnant! I called Irma, first thing. She was ecstatic and told me that the gift of life was the most precious gift of all. Everyone in the entire community was so happy. Our prayers had been heard. Even to this day, the elders who were there and still alive 30 years later ask me how my son is doing. His due date was June 21, the Summer Solstice.

I went back to my special gynecologists who told me that this was impossible; it had to be an ectopic pregnancy. But it was not. Then they told me that I would miscarry. But I did not. I was so happy. After 32 weeks, my uterus, which was only half developed since birth, filled up and I gave birth. I called Irma and she had ceremonies. The Medicine Man called me and told me to pray with the eagle feathers that he had given me. Despite him being born two months premature, my baby was fine. After a few days in the hospital, we went home, a two-hour drive to the mountains where we lived.

I heard noises on the roof of the bedroom where we all slept. For sure I thought there were raccoons scratching around. My husband went up to see what was going on and he reported that there was a bunch of big black birds up there. The noises on the roof went on for many days.

One day, I wanted to read Anna a story and we had a children's bookcase under a skylight, so we settled on the couch there. I held my son in the crook of my arm and started to read the story to Anna. Suddenly, the skylight darkened because all these crows were crowding around it. They were pecking at the corners like they were trying to get inside. More and more crows came. I was a bit alarmed and wondered what was going on. Then, suddenly, I thought maybe they wanted to see my son, born of the prayers of their relatives. So, I held him up for them to see. Then gradually, slowly, they all flew away and we never heard them again. I asked Irma about this. She said it was the Spirit Elders performing a Blessingway.

Irma came to visit us and bears started to visit, too. Irma Bears Stops comes from bear spirit medicine. She wanted to see pictures of these bears who visited where the children played in our yard. They played with the balls and had a great old time. A few years later, after Irma passed on, her family gave me a three-foot statue of a standing bear that she always kept next to her bed. I still have it with me.

My whole family went up one year later in August, for the thanksgiving ceremony. It was so much more relaxing than the year before. We brought lots of gifts, which is a traditional practice for a Wopila, a Lakota thanksgiving ceremony. Our son received his Lakota name—Wawiuskinpi Hokshila, which means, "Boy who Brings Peace." He also received a sacred Lakota pipe and a new brother. The Medicine Man had his first son born during the Sundance, a couple of weeks before we arrived.

After two years, Irma instructed me again. She told me it was time for me to do a traditional Lakota ceremony: Wopila Hanblecheya. This is a vision quest ceremony. She told me it was important for me to offer thanksgiving prayers for the amazing gift of life that I had been given.

I believed Irma and was sure she was the main reason that my son had become a reality in my life, so of course I agreed to do this ceremony.

The time for this ceremony is between Pentecost, at the end of May and Summer Solstice. Traditional Lakota people believe that the time of the June berries is the correct time to do this ceremony. New moon time is when one prays for something needed for the community or family. Full moon time is when one would want to give thanks, so I went up to the reservation at the time of the full moon in the beginning of June to give my thanks.

This Hanblecheya ceremony requires a lot of preparation. These are the instructions that Irma shared with me so I would know what was needed and how to participate in this wonderful ceremony. Ideally, a person actually spends one year getting ready for this ceremony.

To start with, there is no need to bring any food or water for the actual ceremony. I sat out on the hill with only the sacred items listed here, all of which are needed to pray with. It is a pure prayer ceremony. I sat alone, without moving, star quilt wrapped around me, on my bed of sage.

In front of me was the altar that the Medicine Man created for me; the 405 tobacco ties protected me, as they encircled the entire space, and in my hands was the sacred pipe, filled with all my prayers.

As a woman, I had to sew a red dress and a star quilt to wrap around myself for the blessings of the ancestors while I was out praying alone all night and all day. I had to make 405 tobacco prayer ties, flags for the Four Directions tied to four different special plants that I had to find and prepare, a large bag full of fresh sage I had picked and cleaned of any weeds or grass (this became the bed of purification that I sat and prayed on during the long hours of my ceremony). I had to find a wild grapevine out in the forest about five feet long, take off the leaves and weave it into a circle, then make another string of 75 tobacco ties to wind around the grapevine; I found and cleaned a coffee can and filled it with mole dirt for the altar. Probably the most important preparation was the offering to Tunkashila I had specially made with traditional Lakota tobacco, tied up with an eagle feather and sinew.

It is essential to take a pipe with your prayers and intentions to the Medicine Man before the ceremony. He will smoke that and interpret your desires before the sweat lodge starts. There will be a purification sweat before any person is put out on the hill to pray in this special ceremony. For that, every participant takes some sweetgrass and an empty pipe along with sacred tobacco to the sweat lodge. Inside the lodge, the Medicine Man will fill the empty pipe with prayers, smudge it with the sweetgrass for good blessings, and sing beautiful sacred prayer songs in Lakota for their intentions and prayers.

Before all this, it is important to prepare the sweat lodge with fourteen marked, special, sacred rocks: seven for the sweat before the Hanblecheya and seven for the sweat after the Hanblecheya. It is great if you can place sage around the fire for people to sit on inside the sweat. Also, it is important to bring a brand-new ladle and bucket filled with good, fresh water for both sweat lodges. Furthermore, it is considerate to supply food for the thanksgiving breakfast that someone from the community will cook for you after you come down from praying, in the morning. (Coffee, eggs, bacon, potatoes, toasting bread, butter, fresh fruit, oatmeal...whatever you want to offer.)

Soon after this entire Hanblecheya ceremony the participant must prepare the Wopila ceremony. This is a thanksgiving ceremony held in the ceremony house, when you have the important responsibility of thanking everyone, including Tunkashila, for your opportunity to pray on the hill and have your prayers heard.

It is also important to provide all the food needed to create traditional Lakota offerings: buffalo stew, wojape, potato salad, fruit salad, cake, iced mint tea (since it is the hot summertime), and any other food you want to offer. Also, this is the time to bring gifts for the Medicine Man, his family, the assistants, the singers and helpers, and all in the community who were there praying in support of your ceremony.

It requires a lot of preparation and Irma taught me how to do it in the most correct, traditional way. But the most important thing she taught me was how to pray after the Medicine Man put me out there all by myself in the wilderness of the South Dakota Badlands, where the coyotes were howling and the snakes were slithering, and the Sundancer ghosts were blowing on their Eagle Bone whistles from years gone by. This is how she taught me about prayer and how to pray:

First are the thanksgiving prayers: give thanks for your parents, because they gave you your life, the most precious thing you could ever receive. (Irma said that even if they abused you, you must thank them for this most amazing gift.) Next, thank your spouse, then each of your children. Then thank your other relatives, your friends, and your world population.

After you thank all the people, you thank the animals, the insects, the plants, the rocks, the waters, and all the Earth and anything else that comes to mind. After that, you can begin to ask for blessings. She warned me not to ask for blessings of my own imagining for other people. If I was not sure of their desires, the best prayer would be for them to have good health, happiness, and that they believe in themselves. Start as you did with the thanksgiving prayers for your parents, then pray for the blessings that they want for themselves, then for your spouse, your children, your relatives, your friends, your Earth, etc. At the very end of all this praying, you can ask for the blessings that you want for yourself.

You do this entire prayer cycle seven times. First to the West, then the North, the East, the South, our Mother Earth, Father Sky, and to Tunkashila, the Creator himself. This is how she taught me to pray.

If you are interested in prayer, I encourage you to practice this prayer technique of giving thanks for everything and then ask for the blessings of happiness and a belief in oneself. This is useful for anyone in the world and for yourself, too. You can perform this prayer anytime, anywhere. I know from experience how helpful it is.

When you perform the prayer correctly in this Lakota Hanblecheya ceremony, it takes all night. It is especially powerful at one unique time—when the birds start singing as they wake up, when the morning star is shining. That is when I always saw the lights blinking around my altar. Irma taught me not to sleep at all during the nighttime. She said that would be a complete waste of all my efforts and preparation. It was very hard not to sleep when I was alone out there by myself, far from civilization in the dark night.

Furthermore, she warned me, you will be tested. When something scary comes, which it often did, point your pipe at it and tell it to go away. I remember on many occasions doing this. Animals, snakes, insects, and otherworldly things, together with lightning and tough weather conditions, would enter close to my space. Then I would take the pipe that I was always holding in my hands and point the stem at it. I would say, "Go Away! Because even though I respect you, I am here praying for good and I do not want anything to disturb me."

I often had amazing and strange visions. The Medicine Man helped me interpret these in the sweat lodge, the morning after the Hanblecheya was over. After he came to get me where I had been praying, we went straight into that nice warm sweat lodge that had been prepared before we arrived. There we would pray and process.

One can participate in this ceremony for four straight nights and days in a row, or for just one night. If you ever decide to do this traditional sacred Lakota Hanblecheya ceremony, be sure to have a qualified medicine man helping you.

I did this ceremony for eighteen years in a row. I remember the year when Irma passed away, in April. I was devastated. I did not know how I could possibly prepare for the ceremony in June without her, but her beloved brother helped me. For the first and only time in those eighteen years, the Medicine Man put me out in sacred ceremony under the wide-open sky. It was a clear night and the moon was brilliantly full. I went out with an extra blanket because it was cold. I remember sitting out there, ecstatic, shivering cold all night long and as happy as I had ever been. She was there, my best friend, together with me.

The next day at the Wopila (thanksgiving ceremony) we all heard her in the corner where she loved to sit, in the dark ceremony house, singing the sacred Lakota songs that she loved so much in her loud, strong Lakota voice. I melted with love for her. I always yearned to hear her singing again, but that was the only time I heard her, because as the Medicine Man explained, a noble person's spirit after death only stays around the Earth plane for one year.

After I had done the Hanblecheya ceremony for sixteen years (four years for each of the Four Directions), the Medicine Man told me that if I wanted to, I could participate in the Sundance ceremony. I had witnessed many of these ceremonies and thought it would be a wonderful, sacred experience to actually participate in one. There were not many white people in the Sundance circle. He told me not to use my pipe or my eagle feathers that had all been gifts to me but to simply be a humble participant, so as a privileged white participant, that is what I did.

This four-day Sundance ceremony is completely different from the Hanblecheya ceremony because it involves the entire community. Instead of praying alone in the wilderness, you are dancing with like-minded friends and surrounded by a supportive community. There is a powerful drum circle where people gather to sing the Lakota Sundance songs, while the dancers are praying and dancing. It is beautiful, starting before dawn with a purification sweat lodge for the dancers.

After that early morning sweat lodge, the Sundancers dress in their ceremonial clothes with a crown of sage, wristlets and anklets of sage, a dress that has been made for the day and barefoot, for a close connection to Mother Earth. Once assembled, the dancers parade in the light of dawn from their camp, over the dewy grass, through the east entrance of the dance grounds and into the Sundance circle. They are led by the Tree Girl, a young virgin who carries the sacred pipe for the ceremony.

After this happens at sunrise, the Sundancers stay in the circle, praying and dancing all day long. In the arbor, outside the circle of the Sundancers, the surrounding community is fed full meals of medicine food at breakfast, lunch, and dinner. The Sundancers, however, after their morning sweat lodge ceremony, where they get one cup of sacred water, dance all day until sunset (with some breaks). Then they take another purifying sweat before sleeping in a tipi out under the stars (or the frequent, shocking lightning storms). They do not eat or drink anything else for four days, except for their two cups of daily water. They have no connection with the outside world, including any family members in the arbor that surrounds them, because they are isolated in the Spirit world. The Sundancers' choice is to pray. Even during the breaks there should be no talking, just praying.

It is an introspective yet joyful time, and it challenges one to be strong. Sometimes it was hot, like 112 °F in the sun during the middle of July. Then our bare feet would start to burn from dancing on the hot grass. But I remembered Irma's teaching: if you feel any discomfort during ceremony, then you are simply not praying hard enough! The Sundance prayers occur in the same order that Irma taught me for the Hanblecheya ceremony and for each of the four days. Flags honoring the Four Directions and 405 tobacco ties are prepared in advance by each dancer.

Sundance is a very powerful ceremony. Just imagine dancing to the Lakota Sundance songs, with the drumming pounding in your ears and continuing with the rhythm in the circle for many hours, not eating anything or drinking much for four days. The dancers transit into another, spiritual world. Since this is a community event, there is a high level of frequency that can be felt. Consequently, miracles often occur during these four days of ceremony and afterwards, during the course of the following year. Sundance ends with a feast and thanksgiving giveaways from all the people who have completed their four-year commitments. I completed this ceremony after eight years at the age of 68 and I had the best giveaway ceremony that I could contribute.

I feel extremely happy after receiving so many gifts and blessings from my times with the amazing and wonderful Lakota people. I pray that they strengthen their traditions and live their lives filled with happiness and a belief in themselves to fulfill all their dreams.

Despite all my ceremonial times and spiritual experiences with the Lakota people, when I began to write this book about some of my visions in other dimensions, I did not realize they were actually shamanic experiences. I had heard of shamanism of course, but never considered it to be part of my own cultural legacy. What I have learned is that everyone has the potential to be a shaman, as shamanism is simply the intent to engage with the Divine in nature in order to receive messages, power, or medicine.

Shamanism has been around for possibly 60,000 years, based on the information that comes to us from ancient cave paintings. It has survived as a practice all this time, presumably because it is a helpful way to retrieve wisdom from all of time and space in order to help individuals and communities, and even the world. The word shaman means "to see with the heart."

This was exactly my intention when I went out to the wilderness, enjoying the grandeur of nature. For the most part, I did not drum or dance, smudge, sing, or do any psychedelic medicine ceremonies, which are all common shamanic methods that are used to flash into the awakened state. I simply did not know any better. Neither was I selected by a community to do this work for them. Instead, I found myself in powerful locations here on Earth with the intention to enter the spirit realm and to visit with the animals, plants, angels, insects, light energies, rainbows, crystals, and stars, all of whom I considered my friends and allies. Usually in a state of meditative trance, I journeyed to otherworldly realms, which initiate from right here on our Earth. There, I received messages and healing beyond my wildest dreams.

I allowed myself to surrender absolutely, letting myself be taken wherever I was to go, not understanding why or where. I discovered a level of reality that was completely novel, beyond anything ever imagined before. During my visions, I could not actually comprehend the enormity of the beings that I was with. However, I never felt manipulated. I only felt an extraordinary light of pure joy.

I have spent a few years pondering my excursions in order to integrate my experiences. Hopefully, I can assist others who may find themselves in similar situations so they can try to understand their own journeys. My wish is that the following stories will whet your own appetite for discovery and enlightenment.

Welcome to the Magic!

Travels in Mt. Shasta

Mt. Shasta is a phenomenal place that most people have heard of, but few have visited. The massive volcanic mountain erupts out of the towering pines of the pristine Shasta Trinity National Forest in Northern California. It has been considered a sacred place since the beginning of time. Visiting it is like taking a pilgrimage to a vast outdoor cathedral. Similar to the wonderful lenticular clouds (comparable in appearance to flying saucers, which are said to fly high in the sky around the mountain) that often cloak the summit, the mountain itself is shrouded in legends and stories that lend a mystique to the entire area.

Mt. Shasta rises to more than 14,000 feet in solitary isolation, towering above everything around it and creating a massive statement. For eons, Native Americans perceived this mountain as holding the power of God. It has been considered so sacred that, out of respect, indigenous people would not live on the actual mountain. For them, it is a place reserved for important ceremonies. This is where they went when it was time to move on to the next world. The Wintu, Karuk, and Pit River tribes still use the area for ceremonies. Their use of the land for sacred ceremony is honored and respected by the National Forest Service and other government agencies.

Similar to a place like Sedona, Arizona, Mt. Shasta has innumerable energetic vortices up and down its slopes and in the surrounding areas. These energy centers, which are special places where the spirit of the mountain seems especially palpable, are not mapped out. This quality of remoteness gives individuals a unique opportunity to be in powerful places for private meditations, performing the deep inner work that is necessary to have a profound transformational experience—one that often entails traveling to other dimensions. When a person encounters these sorts of energetic vortices on our Earth, it becomes easy to have experiences that are energizing, nurturing, and balancing. It is always an opportunity to create a euphoric connection to the Divine. Often, seekers will receive clarifying messages, healing, guidance, and a wonderful sense of renewal in these powerful vortices.

Just like our bodies, Earth reportedly has at least seven chakras or energy processing centers. It has been established that the first one, the root chakra of our Earth, is located at Mt. Shasta. This means that the mountain is especially helpful in enabling us to release negative energies. The very first chakra is the one closest to the Earth. Being at this site allows us to be in the strongest position to act as a conduit for all the healing energies coming up from the center of Gaia.

There are countless secrets in Mt. Shasta, and they can only be discovered by actually being there on the mountain. Reading about such a place can never be a substitute for the direct experience of the wild, universal life force energy, colorful meadow flowers, cleansing mists of the waterfalls, sparkling spring waters, deep blue sky traversed by clouds full of messages, and glistening white snowfields of Mt. Shasta. I feel blessed to have had the opportunity to go there. I am aware of the power of traveling to a place that has such a strong ability to impact my conscious evolution.

I vividly remember arriving at Mt. Shasta late in the afternoon. My companion and I went downtown to the Visitor's Center to get our bearings. Then we went into one of the iconic shops scattered throughout the quaint little town. I was fascinated by the beautiful crystal singing bowls made from different elements and gemstones (gold, platinum, diamond, ruby, etc.). The owner had hundreds of bowls in her shop in a variety of colors, sizes, and sounds.

I bought a couple of items as they were closing for the day and she invited me, along with a shaman from Australia who teaches something she calls Feminine Law, to stay for a demonstration of the singing bowls.

For half an hour, she showed us how she can use these amazing crystal bowls to create magic. I learned a number of important things from her demonstration, such as how it was possible, with appropriate follow-up, to heal the masculine/feminine relationship, the Earth/Sky connection, the head/heart dichotomy, and much more. The sound of the bowls was so lovely to listen to that by the end, I felt completely uplifted, rested, relaxed, and happy.

Then, out of the blue, the owner told me that according to certain teachings, "Enthusiasm equals wisdom." In fact, *enthusiasm* literally means "God within you." She herself was quite enthusiastic, so I listened on. She proceeded to teach me how to use my standing body as a pendulum. This practice, she explained, was helpful in determining situations and options that might be good or bad for oneself. It was certainly fun meeting people in Mt. Shasta.

In the morning, my companion and I met with a gentleman who lived in the area and would be our guide. First, he took us to Fairy Falls, a lovely waterfall, as magical a place as it sounds. He led us through a short meditation on gratitude and renewal while we were there. We then dipped our crown chakras into the cool, pure water, and I sat in the energetic mist of the falls as it blew through me. I felt cleansed, renewed, refreshed, relaxed, and elated. Along with the butterflies and diminutive flowers, I could sense the beautiful presence of the fairies.

Our guide informed us about some other places to go. One was Sand Flats, up on the flank of Mt. Shasta, which became our next destination. (It might get its name from a sandy area at the bottom from where the land slopes up, just as you enter the region.)

After all this preparation, I had the most amazing vision at Sand Flats. I went up on the side of a rocky knoll where the Medicine Wheel awaited me.

The Medicine Wheel is a monument constructed from stones and laid out in a pattern oriented to the Four Directions. I chose a spot with a view of the snowy slopes of the mountain and sat there watching the clouds form and re-form over Mt. Shasta. I was alone now, with only the birds giving me instructions and the soft breeze sending love across the meadow. After some time, I began to feel the presence of some special, extremely large white beings floating down into the sandy meadow. I sensed they were angelic in nature, and I asked my guides to come and be with me, to help me connect with whatever I was supposed to experience.

Soon, my beautiful, gigantic white angel—a guide that often accompanies me—was at my left shoulder. I generally feel her presence and see and experience her with my inner eye. After a bit, she gathered me in her soft, loving arms and before I knew it, the other beings that were present took the form of large, flowing white angels as well. We all started softly dancing together, floating around in a tall circle. We slowly drifted higher up on the mountain. It was joyous fun. After a while, we began to form a spiral above the mountain. The spiral extended high into the clouds. Gradually, we reversed direction and began to spiral down, directly into the mountain.

As I could see down inside the mountain, I was overwhelmed by the beauty there: luscious gardens, brilliant green trees, and iridescent rivers. The angels became very small; once we were all down inside the lush fairyland of the mountain, I could see that the angels had become fairies that took on appearances in every color of the rainbow. They formed a line of graduated crystalline colors, each holding hands with the color before them. We were one long line of vibrant, undulating colors in rainbow order, and I was at the end.

The Magic of the Real World

We floated just above the ground, over hills and down babbling brooks. The bright fairies showed me their beautiful world as we wound around through the woods and meadows. We came to a magical garden full of vividly glowing flowers. There was a brilliant stream full of crystals, light and sparkling, clear, pure water. The fairies told me to lie down in the stream, so I lay on my back in the light-filled water and crystals. I began to feel a deep connection to Mother Earth. In fact, I felt like I was an integral part of Gaia, lying there with the effervescent golden bubbles, sparkles of crystals, and clear, light-filled water flowing over me, through me, and all around me.

As I lay there, anchored in the Earth, my heart chakra—which is the seat of compassion, empathy, love, and forgiveness—began to open, as it has before in such situations. Many times, I have experienced this exquisite heart opening by seeing and feeling a diamond flower in my heart space. On this occasion, I could feel that a chrysanthemum was beginning to bloom there. This heart flower was made up of thousands of small crystal petals of a pale light blue hue. The chrysanthemum grew bigger and rounder with more petals and more crystals, as it spread out wider than my body.

Lying there, a part of the pure water system of Earth, the mountain above me opened up. I could see that it was nighttime and the stars were abundant in the sky. The stars reflected the crystals in my heart, sparkling with millions of small, glimmering lights. I was part of the galaxy of stars and the stars were part of me, as we shone back and forth. I could easily connect because I knew I was part of the Earth and part of the Sky.

After absorbing this crystalline connection for some time, a Lakota medicine man whom I had met before came into my vision and gently told me it was time for me to get up and take the form of a standing stone. He helped me rise up and found a place for me to be still, in quiet prayer, so I rose up out of my crystal stream bed and became a standing stone, as old as all time.

First, I acknowledged the Four Directions, in fond recollection of my Native American teachings. Then, as if reviewing my life, I noticed every mark on my stone. I saw growing marks from when I was young, as well as scars from my middle years, and smoother parts from older, wiser years. I slowly began to grow taller and taller. After a while, I was so tall that I was coming out of the mountaintop. As the top part of my stone body came out of the mountain, I burst into the powerful sunlight. The sight of the beautiful golden Sun made me so very happy that in order to greet it properly, I turned into a giant sunflower, laid wide open at the summit of the mountain.

Lying there in the fresh, warm, sunlit air, I began to feel and see tiny children with transparent wings alighting on each one of my seeds. There they danced lightly and joyfully. After a large number had gathered, they began to spiral around, following the inward design of my seeds. When they formed a tight little group in the middle, I protectively gathered my petals up around them and took them with me down into the mountain for the night.

In the morning, I pushed up through the hole in the mountain and opened my sunflower petals wide. The tiny, winged children came spiraling back out, once more following the spiral form of the seeds. After dancing around airily on the seeds for a while, they flew off and away. Each time, they left me to wonder about the golden ether that was pervasive. This happened four times. After four days and nights of this fun activity, I grew to love these darling little beings. I wanted to know where they went flying off to.

However, the third dimension was calling me home from this magnificent vision, which seemed to span several days. I heard that it was time to go. I was finished for now.

Pondering Notes

The entire experience at Mt. Shasta was a teaching from our great Mother Earth. These visions occur when we feel serenity, purity, and peace inside the heart.

Spiraling

The connection with the gigantic angels showed how unlimited we can be during our lives here on Earth. Standing in a circle as I did with them evoked a sense of wholeness. Spiraling with the angels helped me to understand how the cosmos creates itself in vortex motion. It produces healing by expanding and contracting, pushing energy out and pulling it in again: masculine and feminine, creating a womb-like condition for a new cycle.

This ensures balance because if we only expand out, we will bust through our boundaries and create imbalance, a condition that we can recognize happening all around us. Earth is a pulsating frequency of light. There are endless dimensions, like circles within circles.

Rainbows

The rainbow fairies each represent a different frequency of sound and light. They love sharing their respective colors of healing energy. They are always flowing, just as they did in my vision, floating up and down through the flower meadows. Their light is a vibration that recharges itself. Rainbow energies have been on our planet since time immemorial; they were here before we came and will be here after we are gone. Their presence helps us to remember the interfacing of different colored frequencies; they can create a breakthrough experience for people to heal and realize new understandings.

We are rainbow healers. Rainbow rays all belong to one divine origin. However, they each have their own unique set of gifts and ways to guide us. In some indigenous spiritual practices, the individual rays are characterized in the following ways:

Red: Well-being and vitality.

Orange: A light for the soul to shine; grounding for harmony and inner peace.

Yellow: Clarity, freedom, abundance in happiness, prosperity.

Green: Healing, awakening, awareness of service to others.

Blue: Clarity as to where you are going and coming from, no confusion or doubts, absolute truth.

Indigo: New consciousness, evolution of consciousness, joy, celebration, completeness.

Violet: Forgiveness that produces change, yielding transformation; making the best of everything through your choices.

Light Blue Crystal

The light blue crystal in the heart represents an opening to higher ideals and principles. I felt grateful to receive this opening, as I believe we are always striving for higher levels of understanding, a new process, and an improved life.

Stone People

Standing stones provide information for the Earth and for humans. I remember the power in the stones at Stonehenge and in the sweat lodge and many other places around our Earth. Consider that even a simple stone contains amazing messages for all of us. When we can become one with a standing stone, we become one with the Stone people. This connection with the stone allowed me to review my life in a supportive, helpful way. In Maya, the word for stone is *tun*. The truth, according to the Maya, is that we are each a precious stone; we just need to be polished. However, they further believe that a stone always gives its light, the light is always with us.

Sunflowers and Seeds

Sunflowers are radiant light, representing a brilliant language of communion beyond words. Their swirling colloidal patterns inform our future, because change is created through spiraling. Sunflowers are an important symbol for the Native Americans who revere their design. It is interesting to note that they always face the sun.

My intention at the top of the mountain was to show up as my best self to the celebration with our Father Sun. I was surprised to enjoy the delightful insect children who came dancing on my seeds. The seeds represent abundance and joy with the potential to fertilize, grow, bloom, feed us, and provide for new life. One can actually rebirth oneself with seed energy. Every seed has a heart. We need to eat and receive the love from each one of the seeds.

Bees, Insects, and Ceremony

The tiny, winged beings are always gathering pollen from sacred flowers to disperse across the Earth. This is etheric pollen, which they distribute to babbling streams, tall forests, singing birds, wise animals, and all people to encourage harmony, balance, and flow. This concept offers us the capacity to self-pollinate ideas. The golden etheric glow is a good indication of hope and better things to come.

Flying insects that join with us in ceremony are beings of light. I have often enjoyed the company of dragonflies and butterflies during ceremonies. They vibrate with genuine love, which is why I adored having them with me.

Spirals and Chakras Meditation

To access a video recording of the meditation, scan this code:

In this meditation, we will go within our bodies to connect with each of our seven chakras in order to expand our energy fields. Chakra is an ancient Sanskrit word for "energy wheel." We will strive to create more inner energy, which is our inner aliveness, by moving spirals around our chakras.

A spiral represents a connection to the Divine, especially in terms of the evolution and growth of our spirits. Spirals can be found everywhere throughout the galaxies, the oceans, and our precisely ordered Earth. This is because they are the most efficient shape requiring the least amount of energy to function. It is important to note that they bring balance by connecting the outer world to the inner soul.

Found throughout nature, we can see spirals in fragile green fern buds, big yellow sunflowers, powerful blue ocean whirlpools, delicate orange shells, indigo star galaxies, blooming red roses, and violet lotus flowers floating in water. These are the spiral pictures that we will use in our chakra meditation. We will start our meditation with the green of the heart chakra and spiral from there.

To start our meditation, get into a comfortable position. Lie down with your back on the ground or sit up, whichever you prefer. Make sure that you are comfortable with pillows and whatever you need for the duration. Now, take a deep breath in, and as you exhale, feel yourself sinking into the warmth of the Earth. Take a few more deep breaths in and out, and slowly feel yourself connecting closer to Mother Earth. Feel the Earth holding you, supporting you. Relax as you breathe in and out.

Begin to focus on your heart chakra in the middle of your chest. Inhale into this space, drawing in fresh energy. Exhale. Inhale again and slowly exhale, allowing the pure energy to settle into this space. Relax. Inhale deeply and slowly...feeling the enormous amount of LOVE that is coming into your heart space. Exhale. Breathe in and slowly breathe out. Allow your heart to open and expand even more. Feel the gratitude that you have in this heart chakra and the happiness there. As you inhale, begin to see a fragile green fern bud spin in your heart space. You can do this by simply being within your body, looking outward. The fern is rotating clockwise and you can recognize its spiral pattern. Enjoy the wonderful green color of the fern filling your heart and spinning. Relax as you envision the green energy rotating like a wheel around in your heart chakra, expanding and filling up the space with Love in your chest. Enjoy this open state of your heart chakra and the vibrant green love energy.

Expand this energy all the way out to the very reaches of the chakra space in your body to both sides of your chest. Welcome this expansion of beautiful green energy. Continue breathing and spinning the entire loving, green space at a comfortable and balanced pace.

Take a breath in and put your focus out to the left side of your chest. Breathe out, down the left side of your chest, around the bottom of the heart chakra, up the right side of your heart, and over the top, in a circular pattern. Now, send your breath in a curved half-circle down the left side of your body and around, over the top of the solar plexus chakra in the middle of your abdomen, around and down the right side. Energy is now entering into your solar plexus chakra. Begin to focus on this. Inhale into this space, drawing in more fresh energy. Exhale. Inhale again and slowly exhale, allowing the energy to settle into your solar plexus chakra.

Relax. Allow this chakra to open and expand more.

As you inhale, begin to see a beautiful yellow sunflower with its spiral of seeds in your solar plexus space. It turns clockwise like a wheel. Exhale. Enjoy the wonderful bright yellow color of the sunflower filling your solar plexus, spinning around. Feel this chakra begin to clear all judgment, just accepting what is. Continue to expand the energy in this space.

Understand that you are being filled with a special inner power. Relax as you envision the bright yellow energy with all its petals rotating in your solar plexus chakra, gradually filling up your upper abdomen's space. Enjoy this open state of your solar plexus chakra, absorbing good energy with the vibrant yellow sunflower.

Now expand this yellow energy all the way out to the very reaches of this chakra space. Feel the energy helping to balance this center. Continue breathing and spinning the entire bright yellow space at a comfortable and balanced pace. Focus on the right side of your upper abdomen. Feel the spiral energy curve around the bottom of the sunflower, up the left side and over the top, back down to the right.

Now inhale deeply, and as you exhale, send your breath in a curved half-circle up the right side of your body under your throat chakra, to the left side, and over the top of it. In this way, you can begin to feel the spiral energy growing inside your body like a flowering vine with its own intelligence.

Begin to focus on your throat chakra. Inhale into this space, drawing in fresh energy. Exhale. Inhale again and slowly exhale, allowing the energy to settle into this space. Relax. Inhale deeply and slowly exhale away all anxiety. Allow this chakra to open and expand more. As you inhale, begin to see a huge blue ocean whirlpool spinning clockwise in your throat space and you can recognize the spiral energy in it. Exhale. Enjoy the wonderful blue color of the ocean whirlpool as it fills your throat chakra, spinning around and clearing all fears. Relax as you feel the blue energy rotating around in your throat chakra, expanding and filling up the space, allowing you to speak your truth. Enjoy this open state of your throat chakra and the vibrant blue energy, clearing your voice.

Now expand the energy all the way out to the very reaches of this chakra space in your neck. Continue breathing and spinning the entire space at a comfortable and balanced pace. Take your breath and your focus to the right side of this space. Now inhale deeply, sending your energy under the throat chakra to the left side of your body. Exhale and send it down the left side to where the sacral chakra is in the lower abdomen. Have that energy curve over the top and around to the right side of it.

Begin to focus on this sacral chakra. As you place your attention on this area in the lower belly, inhale into this space, drawing in fresh energy. Exhale. Inhale again and slowly exhale, allowing the energy to settle into this space. Relax. Allow this chakra to open and expand more. As you inhale, begin to see a perfect orange shell from the sea, spinning in your solar plexus. It is spinning clockwise. Exhale. Enjoy the wonderful orange symmetry of the spirals in the shell filling your solar plexus as it spins around.

Feel this chakra begin to clear. Relax as you envision the orange energy rotating like a wheel around in your sacral chakra. Gradually, it clears out all impurities and fills you with inner strength in the space of your lower abdomen. Enjoy this open state of your sacral chakra and the lovely orange energy. Feel the energy helping to balance this center.

Now expand this energy all the way out to the very reaches of the chakra space in your body. Take your focus from the right side to under the chakra in your lower abdomen. Rotate it up the left side, over the top to the right side. Now inhale deeply, and as you exhale, send your breath in a curved half-circle up the right side of your body to the third eye chakra. The spiral energy moves under the 3rd eye chakra to the left side and up, over the top.

Begin to focus on your third eye, between your eyebrows. Inhale into this space, drawing in fresh energy. Exhale. Inhale again and slowly exhale, allowing the energy to settle into this space. Relax. Inhale deeply and slowly exhale. Allow this chakra to open and expand more. As you inhale, begin to see an indigo galactic spiral, full of planets and stars in your third eye space. It is spinning clockwise. Exhale.

Enjoy the wonderful indigo color of the galaxy with all the distant stars filling your third eye chakra and spinning around powerfully. Relax as you envision the indigo galaxy energy whirling like a wheel around in your third eye chakra, expanding and filling up the space. Enjoy this open state of your chakra and the powerful indigo energy, opening your inner vision. You begin to understand what this opening means for you. Continue breathing and spinning the entire space at a comfortable and balanced pace.

Now expand this energy all the way out to the very reaches of the chakra space in your forehead. Take your breath and your focus down the right side of your forehead, around and under your third eye in a circular pattern to the left side. Now inhale deeply, and as you exhale, send your breath in a curved half-circle down the left side of your body all the way to your root chakra at the base of your torso, over the top of it, and over to the right side.

Begin to focus on this root chakra at the base of your body. Inhale into this space, drawing in fresh energy. Exhale. Inhale again and slowly exhale, allowing the energy to settle into this space. Relax. Allow this chakra to open and expand more, as it is letting go of all fear. As you inhale, begin to see the spiral as a beautiful red rose in your root chakra space. It is spinning clockwise. Exhale. Enjoy the wonderful deep red color of the rose filling up your root chakra space as it spins around. The red color helps you to feel stronger. Feel this chakra being filled with perfume and expanding even more. Relax as you envision the red rose rotating around in your root chakra, gradually filling up the space with its special energy of stability. Enjoy this open state of your root chakra and the powerful red energy.

Now expand this energy all the way out to the very reaches of the chakra space. Take your breath and your focus from the right side, under the chakra to the left side, over the top, curving around and up the right side of your entire bodily chakra system in a half-circle to your crown chakra at the top of your head. It curves under the crown chakra, to the left side, over the top, and onto the right side.

Begin to focus on your crown chakra. Inhale into this space, drawing in fresh energy. Exhale. Inhale again and slowly exhale, allowing the energy to settle into this space. Relax. Inhale deeply and slowly exhale. Allow this chakra to open and expand more, eliminating all confusion and allowing for more clarity. As you inhale, begin to see a violet lotus flower spinning clockwise around on top of your head. Exhale. Enjoy the wonderful violet with the spiral form of its petals filling up the space in your crown chakra. Enjoy this open state of your chakra and the powerful violet energy.

Now you are connecting to a brilliant ray of Light, pouring down from the heavens into the top of your head. You feel this light pulsating there in your crown chakra, filling you with an illuminated consciousness. Expand the energy all the way out to the very reaches of the crown chakra space at the top of your head.

Breathe in. Breathe out. Relax and take some time to enjoy the spirals that you have created throughout your body by revisiting each chakra and rest in this powerful space. Breathe in and breathe out several times. Feel the expansiveness throughout your entire body. Breathe in, breathe out.

Now we will spin back through each of the chakras, ending at the heart chakra, drawing the fields of energy back in. This will not close your chakras, but it will create boundaries for you. This is important so that you do not spin out of control.

From the crown chakra, inhale the energy from the right, circle around the bottom, to the left side. Now, exhale down the left side all the way to the root chakra. Inhale under the bottom of it and around the entire chakra to the right side and exhale up to the third eye chakra.

Inhale and go over the top, down the left side, around the bottom, and circle back over to the left side of the third eye.

Spirals and Chakras Meditation

Exhale, on down to the sacral chakra.

From the left, inhale under the bottom of your sacral chakra and around the entire chakra to the right side, and exhale up to the throat chakra.

Inhale over the top at the throat, down the left, around the bottom and circle back over to the left side of the throat, and exhale down to the solar plexus chakra.

From the left, inhale under the bottom of the solar plexus and around the entire chakra back over to the right side and exhale up to the heart chakra.

Spin the energy around the green of the heart chakra for a little while as you feel the difference in your body energies. Continue to breathe deeply and relax.

Now ask yourself a few questions:

Do you feel that your chakras continue to spin?
Can you feel the balance in your body?
Can you realize the increased energy?

You will have more energy. You will be able to carry all of this out into the world. You are mirroring a microcosm of the unfolding Universe.

Breathe in, breathe out. Feel grateful and give thanks.

This spiral that you formed in your body has created a link between the inner and outer worlds. You are now connected to the Earth and all Beings. Rest here.

Feel the weight of your body on the warm Earth. Spend a few moments feeling the Love from Mother Earth. Reach up with your hands. Wiggle your toes and rotate your ankles. Stretch your body slowly upwards. Open your eyes. Enjoy the rest of your beautiful day and night.

Sunrise

Here he comes, our sacred Sun
Ribbons of sunrise unwrap our gift.
Brilliance, from the beginning of time
Spreads across fields, like a wind shift.

When Father Sun rises in you and me
We awaken to love and we see
Giving is embraced freely,
Co-creation manifests purely.

Focus to enlighten ourselves—
This is when we feel the warmth.
Seek opportunities to transform
All our lives and Gaia, Earth.

Sunlight heals our hearts and souls
Brightening renews from this source.
Cycles of time begin and end
And liberation is brought forth.

Medicine of the kingly Presence
Yields the harvest of many Presents.
By following the Golden Rule
We live in good attendance.

Search For Panther Springs

Strapping on my hiking boots, I was full of excited anticipation to finally see Panther Springs. I had read how Guy Ballard encountered St. Germaine at this spring in 1930, and from that and further encounters developed the "I Am" movement, which came to have a worldwide following. I had waited a long time for this opportunity.

In town, my friend and I asked how to get there and were told that anybody could do this by simply following Panther Springs Creek up the middle of Upper Panther Meadow to the head of the stream, so we drove up the mountain in our rented Subaru with eager anticipation. At Bunny Flats, a well-known trailhead on the mountain, we parked along with everyone else. We had to park there because the road was closed further up, due to massive quantities of snow. Almost everyone was there to climb up to the peak of Shasta and/or ski down the mountain. Remember, this was in the middle of July.

We trudged up the snowy, closed road. The first couple we met were on their way back down. The lady declared in a disappointed voice, "There is a lot of snow." I nodded, thankful for my new waterproof boots. Soon we understood exactly what she was talking about. The next and last person we met coming down was a lady wearing a flamboyant hat. From beneath the hat flowed a long lavender scarf. She was chatting happily on her cell phone, telling someone how cool it was to be on Mt. Shasta. For the next mile and a half, the road was completely covered with several feet of snow and it was empty of people. As we continued, we finally noticed the sign on the right side of the road, barely sticking out of the snow. It read Panther Meadows.

Our directions indicated that we should take the steep road down to the right and wind through some trees; this path would take us to Lower Panther Meadows. There, we would see a path through the trees; Upper

Panther Meadows would be only a short distance away. We would see the creek and follow it up the middle of the meadow to the spring. However, with all that snow, there was no road, no path, no creek, and no people to ask. We were lost.

We plowed through the trees, heading upwards and south until we saw a butte (an isolated hill with steep sides and a flat top) and a large field of snow that covered the meadow. We were still looking for some sign of the spring. We located what must have been a stream bed, judging from its position at the bottom of the draw in the big open field. Of course, there was no running water for a stream, just several feet of snow. We trudged up and down through snow fields, still faithfully searching for the spring.

Finally, I realized we would not find the fabled spring on this trip. We had already been hiking through the snow for three hours. That's when I decided instead to find a place to commune with the beings of the mountain that Mt. Shasta is famous for.

I was feeling very much at peace and happy, and my companion agreed to come back in two hours to find me at a particular rock at the top of a rockslide, the only place where the snow had melted away.

I settled myself very comfortably into spaces among the sharp rocks and became full of the sounds of all the lovely birds. I could also clearly hear the sound of a running stream. However, there was no visible sign of the stream.

Pondering the idea that I would not be finding Panther Springs on this trip, I asked the beings of the mountain for help in understanding whatever there was for me to understand. I did point out to them that I had gotten myself up there on a weekend in the middle of July and that nobody else was there besides my companion, who had agreed to leave me alone for two hours. Despite my plea for communication, nothing happened for what seemed like hours, except for the singing yet still birds and the invisible running stream.

Finally, as I sat in meditation, my big, beautiful white angel, who can hold me in the palm of her hand if she wants to, came and lovingly gathered me up in her embrace and told me that she would show me the spring at Panther Meadows.

Search For Panther Springs

She held me up over a meadow; at the head of it was a flowing spring. From the spring came flowers, floating out and up into the sky. There were millions of tiny flowers of every color and every variety, from lilies to roses to wildflowers. Some flowers looked like stars, others like butterflies, still others looked like bells. They continued to come forth out of the spring in an endless flow of beauty and colors and as they came out, they spread apart and grew bigger. This generated a cornucopia effect as the flowers emerged from the spring, small at first, spreading out and getting bigger as they floated up into the sky.

After a while, instead of flowers coming from the spring, out flew white birds, which also grew bigger as they came out. Then newborn babies emerged. Then there was a brown-skinned golden baby that still had its umbilical cord attached to the spring. As the baby came out farther into the sky, the cord got longer and longer. Finally, there was a big bald eagle that came flying out with purpose, deliberately using its powerful wings to fly forward, yellow beak leading the way, a look of determination in its eyes.

My angel then took me to a special place where there were six very large white beings surrounded by white light and standing in a circle. They were not clearly defined because the light was so bright around them. I joined them in the circle. Now we were seven. We stood there for a long time, totally silent and in joyous white light. It seemed that they were summoning healing energies.

Then one of them became what seemed like the same eagle that had flown out of the spring. It was one of the white beings, but it had an eagle head, yellow beak and all. We stood silently in the brilliant white light. I felt a sense of pure ecstasy in the silent presence of these beings. I could have stayed there happily forever.

Finally, the eagle being took off flying and the rest of us fell in behind, so we were in a line of white light that looked like a long cloud. No one on Earth knew we were anything else but a cloud. As we started flying around, it seemed that we were going on a tour of Earth in order to get a big, broad picture of life on Earth. First, we went to the Sundance, a sacred ceremony held by indigenous people to honor Earth and the Ancestors. It was taking place in North America, and we watched and supported all

Search For Panther Springs

those who were inside the Sundance Circle. We knew they were praying very hard for our relatives and our Earth. We circled around four times.

After passing over the equator and going south, we arrived at Machu Picchu, known as the Crystal City of Light, in the shape of a condor. There we saw many shafts of a green light coming down from the heavens, some of which were connecting into people's heads. Several shafts did not connect to any heads, and many heads did not connect with any light. But the ancient city was filled with a beautiful, glowing, golden light. Then we flew over to Lake Titicaca, where we could see an amazing crystal city beneath the waters. This city, which looked like a luminous castle, was not in ruins but was very much alive with energy.

We flew south along the Andes and soon were over Antarctica. There, we could clearly see an opening in the Earth at the South Pole. We entered that hole in a rush of energy and found an intense white light flowing through the center of the planet. It ran all the way through to the Arctic. We journeyed in an exhilarating magnetic spiral of brilliant white light that passed between the poles and came out above the North Pole. There, we circled around and viewed the glaciers.

Next, we recognized our friend, Whale. We knew he was our friend because he waved his great tail at us. Whale invited us to go for a swim with him, so we held on, arms around his big belly. We had the most fun time, swimming through the oceans and feeling so refreshed and happy. Up and down we went through the waters, just like the dolphins at play, but we were being pulled by Whale. It was a momentous, joyous experience. Whale took off into the sky, and we went circling around a most amazing mountain.

The mountain had a lot of snow and beautiful energy. There went Whale around the mountain with all of us holding on, so it looked as if Whale had a long white tail. We cherished our time around this beautiful mountain.

Search For Panther Springs

Whale went diving back into his oceans with such a big kersplash, we all went flying in separate directions. I found myself surrounded by drops of water turning into twinkling diamonds. All around me were these sparkling diamonds, and I soon realized they were actually stars. I was floating in the dark universe among millions of twinkling stars. It was very beautiful.

After a while, I began to wonder why I was there. I waited for an answer. Slowly, I began to feel a bit lost. I realized that I had drifted too far away from the protective energy of our Earth and solar system. I asked for help. My angel came right away and scooped me up in her big, loving arms. Then I heard the crunch of snow. It was my companion's boots coming through the snow to get me. I had been there for two hours. We drank some water and prepared to leave.

On the way back, my friend wanted to show me something. He had spent the time during the two hours that I was alone looking for Panther Springs. I explained to him that I had already seen the spring and that I was fine with not exploring further. But he led me up the valley to show me what he thought was the correct location. There was no stream, no spring, only piles and piles of snow. But he took me to a spot and said he was sure that it started around there somewhere. I looked up and saw four white tobacco ties and flags to the Four Directions hanging in the trees.

They were tied so high up, I could not figure out how anyone had reached that height to tie them on at the tippy ends of the spruce branches. However, I have seen amazing things happen with tobacco offerings, so I did not ask any questions. By then I knew that my friend was correct. Panther Springs had to be around there, nearby.

Search For Panther Springs

Pondering Notes

Flowers

This journey was a huge adventure filled with hope, light, and love. It felt perfect that when it finally started, after a few delays, it started with flowers. Flowers are a beautiful part of our creation, each holding a million blessings. Once when I was in Bolivia, a shaman explained to me that when we cup our hands over an open flower, we can receive all the blessings of the universe, as well as eternal happiness.

Some believe that each of the chakras (the seven energy centers in our body) is actually represented by different colored flowers. To take a bath in flower water is cleansing, purifying, and effortlessly transforms bad energy into good. Furthermore, when we step into a circle of white flowers with the right intention, it is possible to renew our life. Imagine that!

White Birds

The white birds flying out of the spring could represent the doves of peace. They symbolize pure transcendent energy, and they could be messengers between worlds. The birds that I saw were so full of a high vibration, they may have been angels.

New Babies

The babies being born from the sacred spring represent the hope of life for our new future world. They could be water spirits, representing flow and clarity. These babies were being born from the womb of Mother Earth.

The brown-skinned golden child had an umbilical cord attached to our Mother Earth. Some visionaries have seen this baby as an androgynous image for our future salvation. Many believe that in ancient earthly civilizations from eons past, the beings here were all androgynous. The color brown represents a connection to the fertile soil of Gaia. It enables our soul to be fully integrated into our bodies because Earth's energy includes all the five elements of life: fire, ether, earth, air, and water.

This allows us to fuel ourselves, turning on our electricity and magnetic fields to provide protection, wholeness, and integration. This vision of the brown-skinned baby was a powerful picture of the future potential for a civilization that could be one soul of humanity instead of billions of fractured egos.

Eagles and Clouds

The eagle is connected to all sky gods and the Sun. Flying through the air, it signifies freedom, speed, and a regal nature. When the eagle soars through the sky, it has a broad view, seeing the wholeness of everything. It can carry our prayers to the Sun.

Clouds often represent messages from the heavens. They can look like animals or symbols with many types of messages. We often wonder who or what is in the clouds that pass by.

Sundance

The Sundance is an old, sacred ceremony that is celebrated by indigenous people in North America. I have danced with the Lakota people for many years in this ceremony and can say that it is a profound prayer experience providing a portal into renewed life each year.

City of Light

Machu Picchu, located in Peru, is a city of light. According to some teachers, it was designed to be an advanced school for learning how to use the light of the Three Suns: the Galactic Sun, the Sun we see in the sky, and the Sun energy in our own hearts. Learning about this will allow us to find our power through love, service, and wisdom. Many ancient cities in South America are crystal cities of light, particularly any found deep in Lake Titicaca. The cities there can be seen by the heart and also by advanced divers who can descend into the depths of that high-altitude lake. It is said that this is where the records from Lemuria and Atlantis are kept.

It was beautiful to see the glaciers at the North Pole, covering the crown of the Earth with a bright, white layer of crystal protection. This ice is helping to keep our Earth balanced.

Mt. Kailash

Our friend, Whale, so full of loyalty and love, showed us important things, especially how to have fun and play. The mountain he took us around was Mt. Kailash. For most people in Asia, this is a sacred mountain, and it is shrouded in mystery. At 22,000 feet, it is part of the Himalayas and is located in Tibet. It is said to have supernatural powers and cannot be climbed, even though it is lower than Mt. Everest.

Considered a cosmic axis and a pillar of the world, it is believed by some to actually be an ancient pyramid with two cities buried underground at its base. This mountain that Whale flew us around is considered the crown chakra of Earth. The crown chakra is the seventh chakra of a body, be it human or our actual Earth. It represents spiritual connection and transformation, connecting us to the Divine.

Traveling Through the Universe

Traveling into the dark universe represents pre-human birth and coming from the stars. It was amazing and brilliant for me to be with the stars. However, it is important not to travel too far from our solar system, where we are protected by our Mother, the Earth, and our Father, the Sun. There are forces beyond this protection that could harm us. That's what I felt when I called for help. I was so grateful for my guardian angel, who brought me home.

Tobacco Ties and the Four Directions

Tobacco is a sacred medicine among indigenous people. Tobacco ties are offerings to the spirits bundled in cotton fabric and filled with prayers. They are as powerful as our intentions. When medicine people place their tobacco ties on sacred plants, sparks are spontaneously ignited.

Flags to the Four Directions are especially sacred offerings. As I have learned from the Lakota people, the Four Directions represent the four winds—or in the European world, the four ethers.

Starting with the West (Wiyohpeyatakiya), the color is black. This is where the Sun sets, and it represents the end of life and the direction our ancestors come from. The thunder spirits also come from this direction, representing the waters of life, which we cannot live without. This direction brings balance and boundaries. It is represented by the Horse Nation. Horses are sacred to the Native Americans and have been used by them for a long time to promote mental health.

Next, the Lakota honor the North (Waziyatakiya), and the color is red. This direction features the cold, cleansing winds, demanding patience and endurance by the community to face their trials; it also determines the will to live. The direction is represented by the Buffalo Nation.

The direction of the East (Wiyohiyanpatakiya) has the color of yellow, representing the sunrise, a new day, and a renewed life. This direction fosters understanding of what it takes to live a good life, focusing on relationships. It is represented by the Elk Nation and the Deer Nation.

South (Itokagatakiya) is represented by the color white. This is where the renewing, warm winds and life-giving forces come from. Our ancestors journey along the Milky Way to and from this direction during their travels. This direction is represented by the Eagles and the Bird Nation.

When we make flags for these Four Directions with the proper understanding and intention, our prayers are very powerful.

St. Germaine and the Violet Flame Meditation

To access a video recording of the meditation, scan this code:

In this meditation, we will connect with the Ascended Master, St. Germaine, and the Violet Flame, which he works with and has so generously offered to help our world ring with a new sense of freedom. There are many Ascended Masters available to help us today, especially during these troubled times. They each come with a highly evolved frequency and a unique energy. It is a blessing and a privilege to share in their messages.

There is so much darkness upon our Earth now. It is an affliction coming from within us, humans. It has been festering for a long time. It is not coming from our blessed Earth but from a long history of our fears and doubts that have lurked in the darkened corners of our minds for ages. We can feel the epic atrocities and utter devastation that humanity has been responsible for. However, right now we are living in a special interval of time for light workers to claim their rightful spiritual destiny. With the Violet Flame, there is an opportunity for a renewed spiritual energy of love, mercy, freedom, and transmutation that can help us and the whole world. We need to embrace the concept that life is a school where we learn to take responsibility for our own energy.

What exactly is the Violet Flame? It is an invisible spiritual energy that revitalizes us by changing negative energy into energy that makes us joyful. In science, violet light is the shortest wavelength of light. Therefore, it has the highest frequency and the most energy. This means it has the greatest ability to change matter at an atomic level, resulting in the capacity to cleanse, clear, and transmute. It is sometimes called the ceremonial or magical ray because of all these qualities.

During his first revelations about the Violet Flame, Saint Germaine said, "The use of the violet consuming flame is more valuable to you and to mankind than all the wealth, all the gold, and all the jewels of this planet." (*The Voice of the I AM*; January 1941, p. 20.) So we need to learn how to work with this powerful force. We will do so with this meditation.

Ascended Masters like St. Germaine come with a high frequency of energy. It can be easier to meet them in a high-frequency location. Mt. Shasta is one of those places. Indeed, many people, not the least of whom was Guy Ballard (the channel for many of St. Germaine's messages), have encountered St. Germaine and his Violet Flame at Mt. Shasta. While I was there, several times I was humbled to meet St. Germaine and work with his Violet Flame. We intend to take you to Mt. Shasta in a spiritual way and hopefully you too will encounter St. Germaine's brilliance and powerful vibration of love there on the mountain, connecting with the Violet Flame.

Let's start our meditation:

Imagine that you are high up on the flanks of Mt. Shasta. The snow on top is glistening, pure white. You can smell the fresh scent of the pine forest as you look for a place to settle down. You pass by a bubbling creek where the water is running clear and sparkling in the sunshine. All around, colorful wildflowers are blooming in the meadows. Finally, you come to a comfortable spot, away from people. Here you sit down on the Earth and lean against a tree for support. You can hear the birds singing to each other about you. Here you are safe and comfortable. You can relax and trust that all is well. Take a deep breath in and let it go with a deep sigh.

Relax. Now look up in the blue sky toward the golden sun that is shining brilliantly and warming you. You notice that in the middle of the powerful golden sun is a strong white light. Sit with this vision for a while and take a good deep breath in; exhale with a deep sigh. You are now ready to start.

Ask the white light from the sun to come down to you. Invite this pure white light into your heart. Take a breath in. As you exhale, spread the light out from your heart center into your entire heart chakra space, from one side of your chest to the other. Next, ask it to spread even further, out beyond your heart space and all around you. You can envision pure white light all around your body, enveloping and protecting you. Think of yourself as being inside an egg of brilliant white light. Put your hand on your heart and take a deep breath. Welcome this radiant white light into your life, your body, your mind, and your spirit. Feel the protection of Archangel Michael and Saint Germaine around you there. Say a prayer that the light you call upon is used for the blessing, healing, and protection of all life on Earth.

Now that you are filled and embraced with the essence and purity of the brilliant white light, look up into the sky. Floating high above you, you can see the large form of a man dressed in violet robes and surrounded by a violet aura. The violet light is swirling around him. You can see the actual flames of transmutation licking from his feet up his body. This is Saint Germaine. You can feel the love of his energy reaching down to you. You ask to be enveloped by this violet flame so that you can be purified of all destructive and negative thoughts. You want the violet flame to burn out from you all energy that has been misused; all bad thoughts, anger, lies, hate, jealousy, ill-will, sadness, loneliness, sickness—everything that has been used against all of life. You ask for forgiveness. You beg that these things be transmuted by the fiery violet flame.

You feel yourself being lifted in a spiral of white light up into the embrace of Saint Germaine. As you arrive there, you are enveloped by the vibrant violet light. It has filled your entire body, your mind, your spirit, your soul. It has expanded throughout you. You can feel wave after wave of this brilliant violet color washing through you, cleansing every cell, purifying you. The vibrant violet color is all around you. You can feel the flames transmuting the negative energies. You begin to declare: I AM purified. I AM healed. I AM free. I AM in harmony. I AM joyful. I AM loved. I AM whole. I AM transformed!

Enjoy this feeling of wholeness, comfort, and a sense of oneness with all life. Take a deep breath, inhaling the violet flames into your lungs. As you exhale, send this energy out into the world. There is no limit as to how far the violet flame can reach. Direct it all across the Earth. See it saturating everything and every place that is standing in the way of a new day that could be filled with peace and love. Focus on particular family members or friends who may need help. Send them the Violet Flame. Take another breath in and as you exhale, send the Violet Flame out to some place on our Earth that needs healing. You can do this as many times as you wish.

Now we can say this beautiful prayer together:

Heavenly Source of All Being
May the embrace of your Light guide us.
We walk on the way.
May the might of your endless love fill all space and time.
We are the Light of the World.
May the lines of Light open
Connecting all Beings as brothers and sisters.
We are the Union of Light.
May grace fill our voices, hearts, and hands,
Always.

Take some time to feel the impact of this prayer.

Thank St. Germaine for the Power, Wisdom, Love, and Light that he has held for you today. You find yourself slowly leaving the loving embrace of St. Germaine. You spiral back down in the white light to your position on the Earth, leaning against the tree. Take a deep breath, in and out. Send the white light from your heart back to the sun.

It is time to ground yourself, letting go of the high vibration that came from the higher dimensions. Listen to the birds singing and look at Mt. Shasta glistening in the bright sunshine. Put your hands on the ground and feel the Earth's energy, feel the strong tree trunk against your back. Put your arms behind you and give the tree a hug. When you are ready, return to Earth and continue your work of awakening to the Joy and Light that we are all capable of.

DEER PEOPLE

The Deer People are my people.
They come, helping me
In the forest, on the islands,
Through the waters…to be free.

Quietly they step out when
They are ready to be seen.
Soft eyes and gentle spirits
Lead me, grateful to convene.

Guiding me along my path
With ceremony and ritual.
Always there for confirmation—
Ecstasy becomes instinctual.

Effortless, they leap up hills
With spiritual awareness
Toward the Light, reflecting back
And adding to our happiness.

I love them, my Deer family,
These kind beings of Mother Earth.
Energize us with your sage,
Good medicine for our rebirth.

Dolphin Journey

As an introduction to this story, you should know that I was born on Kauai in the Hawaiian Islands. In Kekaha, along the south coast, my bedroom overlooked the Niihau Channel, where many whales pass through in the Winter. Often I heard their songs. They taught me their mantras. As a young girl, I learned these things and it was a special yet natural initiation.

Every morning my Mom, in her wisdom, did the most valuable thing for us children. She took us across the street to the beach. There we learned about the ocean. We found the most amazing shells, some of which I have not seen in such beautiful varieties for a long time. At the beach, we learned about the tides and how everything moves with the little currents and the big currents. So together, with the waves, we learned to move that way, too. It was magical to watch the tiny fish that swim in the miniature tidal pools together with soft sea cucumbers and spiny sea urchins, flowing back and forth with the seaweeds. They were special living coral gardens.

We learned to harvest the seaweed and little snail shells. The local people taught me how to prepare these things to eat, so we harvested from the sea. During storms, the sharks sometimes came into the bigger pools and got trapped there, swimming madly in circles until a high tide allowed them to swim out. Every day was exciting as we watched what was going on from our little spot on the vast Pacific Ocean.

Sometimes there were tidal waves, sometimes hurricanes, sometimes hukilaus, which were harvesting ceremonies from the sea that ended in wonderful community feasts. Oftentimes, there were beautiful sunsets over the island of Niihau.

Some of our happiest times were with the dolphins, who were there to play with us. They always looked so happy, with smiles on their faces, spinning up in the air, traveling together in huge family groups. We loved them and they taught us so much. Actually, I believe that the dolphins taught me how to swim, how to move through the waters and to move together with the force of the water. Here is a story about my time with the beautiful dolphins.

The color was vibrant ocean aquamarine. I stood there in the cool water. Flanking me on either side was a dolphin, much bigger than I was. Their powerful energy tugged at me. After years of swimming competitively and in many ocean waters, I understood how when water started to move in one direction, it had a lot of power to move things along with it—much more power than air, for example. Growing up on the Hawaiian shores and studying the ocean every day, watching how the currents moved and the waves broke, I began to understand the energy of water. Furthermore, after swimming several miles daily while training for the Olympics, I learned how to move my own body through water, using its energy to help me go forward.

I easily recognized that by undulating in the same wave with the dolphins, their momentum could carry me forward—as long as they did not go too fast and leave me behind. I hoped they would take me with them for a free ride. They willingly understood my prayer and away we went. It was sheer ecstasy, riding along with them through the amazing flow of the ocean. I felt a love emanating from them that engulfed me in euphoric bliss.

I remember feeling this way one special time before, when I found myself floating in a huge bubble of brilliant white light, somewhere out in the universe. This same extraordinary sense of profound happiness came over me again.

The dolphins and I journeyed together for quite a while this way and I felt full of a type of pure love that passed all understanding. After some time, they showed me the spiraling tunnels that go from the ocean into Inner Earth, a place that exists under the surface of Gaia (another name for our Mother Earth). We angled down through one of these tunnels. Arriving into this quiet sanctuary, I felt calm and peaceful. We continued swimming in the inner ocean, but it seemed more like a lake.

Dolphin Journey

Slowing down, we saw the iridescent crystalline colors of green, pink, purple, and blue that permeate the lands and seascape deep inside our Earth. These scalar energies are electric and enlivening. Generally, the light is dimmer inside the inner ocean than it is on the surface, so it seemed to showcase the shimmering lights that we glimpsed. Shooting like lightning bolts of brilliant electric colors throughout the spaces, the scene was exquisite and soothing. We could see towering, luminous crystal formations on the land, but we stayed in the water.

The dolphins showed me how the sacred springs we drink from on the Earth's surface bubble up through tunnels from the Inner Earth, bringing forth extraordinarily pure water. We took one of these tunnels up toward Gaia's surface, spiraling through lovely crystals all the way, and found that it emptied into the sacred Lough Gur (a lake considered sacred by the ancient Celts) in Ireland. This is a place I have visited by land. It was uniquely interesting to arrive there by way of the water tunnels from Inner Earth. There are ancient legends of a crystal city deep in Lough Gur's waters, and now I know that these stories are true.

We spiraled back down in the opposite direction via a new fractal pattern of concentric circles; here, the flows of information occur toroidally, spiraling into the soul and back out into new conscious awareness. Next, they took me to another area that I knew from my youth, the springs of water that bubble up south of Kona, Hawaii, in a sacred place called Pu'u Honua O'Honaunau. It is a place that has been sacred since the beginning of time; the ancient Hawaiians declared it a Place of Refuge. It is a sanctuary of forgiveness, where whatever sin you have committed will be forgiven through ritual. This is where true healing happens.

I was grateful to be taken there. I knew the dolphins wanted me to feel the healing. I heard words echo in my ears, "You are forgiven now. Be free, you are forgiven for all." It was a beautiful ceremony that took some time to get through, as I scanned my memory for the things I was holding on to, starting from my youth to more recent days. After a huge release that filled me with tears and grace, we took off, leaping into the waters again with great joy.

My dolphin friends showed me how, while swimming between them, I could send forth a bubble of love. Literally in the water in front of each one of us was a donut-shaped air bubble. Inside of these forms was a pure love that we could bounce forward with our intention and direct to wherever we wanted the love to go. This would travel toroidally any distance until it got to its destination.

It was so much fun and the dolphins had me practice until I really got it down. I hope I always remember how to accomplish this, anywhere, anytime.

After all this, I must have been exhausted, since I suddenly found myself lying on a beach, covered by a wash of pure sand, but not in the water anymore. As I relaxed and lay there in the dim moonlight, through my body came lovely, undulating waves of color.

These were the colors of the rainbow: first red, from my feet, surely from deep down in Mother Earth. The red passed through each chakra and emerged from the top of my head. Next came orange, in the same manner, then, yellow, green, blue, indigo, violet, and white, followed by a pure golden light that flowed back and forth throughout my entire being.

Lying there, enjoying the warm, golden energy inside of me and radiating out all around, I realized that a beautiful flower was opening in my heart, like a huge white, many-petalled chrysanthemum. In the middle of this flower was a clear, sparkling diamond. In my heart, I recognized the spectacular jewel, which was a very bright light.

Half covered in the crystalline white sand, lying on the beach, and staring up into the dark universe, I began to notice, out in the vast darkness, other jeweled lights sparkling, connecting, slowly showing me their love. I realized that I was connecting my light with many other light beings that exist in our cosmos. This was an exhilarating moment I will never forget.

I understand now that the dolphins had prepared me for this entire transfiguration by revealing to me first of all the knowledge of pure unconditional love, just by being in their presence and swimming together with them along the trails of Gaia's waters. Very importantly,

Dolphin Journey

they taught me through the graceful ceremony of forgiveness how to love myself, no matter what. But perhaps most importantly, they taught me how to project love from myself out to the world, to direct it properly, and be persistent in this work. It was a profound experience, full of grace and love that left me dancing with joy. All I can say is thank you to my dolphin friends for this beautiful, amazing journey.

Pondering Notes

Dolphins in the Aquamarine Energy

Being with the pulsating love of the dolphins was like being with the angels. I trusted them completely to take me on this journey; they were so gentle and I felt their love for me and everything else around us. We connected in the water, a comfortable place that I know well, as I have spent a lot of time there throughout my life. The aquamarine color of the water is significant because it is like being inside a crystal of that color. This is a very safe and protected place to be. Aquamarine is also one of the seven sacred colors of the Lemurian Goddesses. Whenever I feel a negative energy, I put myself inside a beautiful aquamarine crystal. Then I feel protected and so much better.

Water

Water has many properties and purposes. It is a powerful clarifying force that encourages flow and enhances intuition. Together, the dolphins and I explored different realms of water: surface ocean, salt water, water from Inner Earth, and fresh spring water. As Dr. Masaru Emoto demonstrated in his book *The Hidden Messages in Water*, water carries wisdom. He illustrated that healing prayers can actually repair the form of frozen water crystals. Water is a self-organizing, harmonizing information carrier. It wants to nourish Gaia because water and Earth are connected, instead of being separate dimensions.

Portals

Spiraling down into Inner Earth as I did with my dolphin friends, created a vortex of life force energy that was purifying. This exercise was a healing that arose from moving through a sacred portal. Whenever you consciously go through a portal, something renews within you.

Mother Earth

To be inside the Earth is a soothing, healing experience. It is like being inside a cave, where the light can be found when you look for it. Crystals come from deep inside Gaia, offering a treasure chest of glittering colors and healing rooms. Some believe this is where Mother Earth's spirit resides—and it is from here that her warmth, love, and energy emerge.

The Mother provides everything we need, free for the taking: all our food and water, the natural beauty of the mountains and waters, rocks and crystals; support for animals, birds, and fish; our trees and flowers. Everything is a gift from our Mother Earth (whom I also refer to as Gaia throughout the book).

We need to remember that she is here to help us. In fact, we are a part of her. Our bones are made of the same minerals as our Earth, our blood and tears run with the same briny taste as the ocean waters. We want to give her gratitude and love every day, so I pray, "Thank you, good Mother Earth, for providing us with everything we need for life. May we repay you by consciously taking better care of all your bounty."

Earth will always take care of life for the animals and plants because they are much older forms of life than we humans are. Gaia, animals, and plants work together to heal and sustain us humans. They will persevere, even if we do not.

Sacred Springs

Springs that we find on the Earth's surface are magical places of pure virginal water surrounded by stories of holy visions and healing forces. The water found in natural springs has been purified and energized by all the crystals it has passed through on its way to the surface. Underwater crystal cities are mentioned in myths from around the world. These are places that live within our hearts and spirits; they are seen by the heart's eye.

Forgiveness and Self-Love

At Pu'u Honua O'Honaunau, where I was taken for the ritual of forgiving myself, I found a portal for removing the obstacles to self-love. This is important because we cannot give what we do not already have. We must love ourselves to be able to love others fully. This is a worthy goal: unconditional love for everything is what makes us happy. This is what sustains us.

Diamond Consciousness

What was the amazing diamond energy in my heart? Diamond consciousness is much more than this world. It is a portal into a new, higher consciousness, a deeper universal wisdom. With everything changing so quickly, it is an important and necessary luminosity for us to experience now. It is a blend of our highest values: love, mercy, understanding, joy, courage, justice, truth, and wisdom. The world is a precarious place, and we need our highest and best to feel more connected to others now by being compassionate, useful, and cooperative.

The diamond appears when you need to make a shift in your life. This is precisely what happened to me as I gained a new level of self-forgiveness. To find out more about Diamond Consciousness, please connect with the work of Donna Eden and her amazing Energy Medicine.

Meditation for Healing in Our Ocean Waters

To access a video recording of the meditation, scan this code:

Now we will go to the ocean for a special healing.

Find, in your imagination, a beautiful white sand beach where it is warm. Go there in your mind's eye.

It is a calm day with a blue sky and the sun shining.

Sit down in the warm sand and feel the soft, warm sand on your legs. Look out at the ocean water and see the beautiful aquamarine color.

Listen to the gentle waves washing up onto the shore and then flowing back into the water. The water rushes up, waits for a silent moment, then flows back again.

Feel yourself breathing…in and out, like the waves. Take a nice deep breath in as a wave washes up.

Exhale deeply as the water recedes back into the ocean, breathing with the sound of the sand and water. Continue breathing with this rhythm for a while.

Feel any tension from your body being released into the warm sand below you. Feel the relaxing touch of the soft sunshine as it caresses your body. It is nourishing and loving you.

Continue breathing with the rhythm of the waves, releasing any tension, feeling the warmth and love all around you.

Now you are ready to get up and slowly walk down to the gentle shoreline. Enjoy feeling the warm, soft sand on the bottom of your feet. Carefully put your toes into the water. It feels good and refreshing. Now, slowly walk into the beautiful clear water. Go at your own pace, feet feeling the sand below, as you get used to the caress of the nice warm water.

You can settle with your feet on the sand below the ocean water, while the rest of you is floating. Your arms are in the water and it feels soothing. The small waves gently rock you back and forth as they come and go. It is very relaxing. Continue breathing… in and out with the rhythm of the waves.

As you allow yourself to be like this—partially floating in the water—you can understand that this is a deep cleansing for your body and your mind. Water can clear away thoughts, ideas, and problems that do not serve you. This ocean water has no judgment of you; it simply observes you, so you can now form the intention to be cleansed of negative energies, thoughts, and forces that may be affecting you. The water will clear it all away. Water can read your thoughts and it is very compassionate.

Continue your deep breathing with the gentle rhythm of the waves. Is there anything that needs to be cleared away in your life? Ask the water to cleanse it away.

What is your biggest challenge these days?

Do you feel sad? Ask the water to help you feel more content about your life.

Are you feeling angry? Ask the water to send you an understanding about the situation.

Do you feel helpless? Ask the water to substitute hopefulness.

Any resentment? Ask the water to replace it with forgiveness.

Are you feeling frustrated? Ask instead for a feeling of satisfaction.

Do you feel annoyed about anything? Ask the water to let you be more accepting.

Are you feeling not good enough or ashamed? Ask the water to send you feelings of thankfulness.

Do you feel afraid of anything? Ask the water to send you more love so you can push away the fear.

Is there any other thought or feeling that you want to clear away? Do that now. After this work, you feel cleansed in your body, mind, and spirit.

Continue your deep breathing with the gentle rhythm of the waves.

Now you can begin to notice the sparkling Light that is reflecting off the water all around you. Water is mostly LIGHT. This is because half of the water on our Earth has come from the sparkling stars. We are each full of water and so we are sparks of the divine light. See the Light all around you sparkling in the water. Feel the Light entering your body through your heart space. Allow it to fill up your heart. Let the light begin to flow from your heart throughout your body. Let it fill up your chest. Feel it flow into your stomach area. Now let the Light flow up into your head. Let your arms and legs be filled with Light. If there is another area of your body that is yearning for more light, ask the water to send it there. Continue your deep breathing with the gentle rhythm of the waves. The water has filled you with Light! You are a Light Being! Enjoy this feeling of purity.

You begin to understand that this water is fluid intelligence. It is the source of divine intelligence. Now you recognize the sacredness of water. We are each full of water and so we are sparks of the Divine. Continue your deep breathing with the gentle rhythm of the waves.

We can communicate with water. Water can share information with us because it is a spiritual teacher. One thing it teaches us is that when we send love out, water receives the love and in turn, sends it to every living being because we are all connected by way of water. This is an important time for us to work with water because water can have a very positive impact on our entire Universe.

Continue your deep breathing with the gentle rhythm of the waves.

Now open your heart and send love out into the water. As you send love out, the water is forwarding this love all around to everything that has water within it, to every living thing. Water expresses its consciousness through you. The more love you send to it, the more it will fill you and everything else with its consciousness of love.

This is how water is a spiritual teacher. It encourages us to be aware of our emotions and the effect they have on everything around us. The more health and happiness we have, the more the Universe has. Water is a connector of all life. Keep breathing, sending love.

Enjoy your time in the warm water with the Light reflecting all around you. Feel the love coming into your whole body, feel the Light in your heart. Remember this joyousness. Keep breathing and sending love and light.

Once you feel completely happy with all your love and light, it is time for one more exercise. When you are ready, take a deep breath and gently put your head under the water. Feel the protection of the aquamarine water all around you. Feel the unconditional love that surrounds you, the Light that is pouring into you. Remember this feeling for later. If you ever need spiritual protection, use your imagination and put yourself into an aquamarine crystal. There you will be protected.

Come up for a breath of fresh air.

It is time now to slowly stand up and walk out of the gentle waves toward the shore. Sit back down in the warm sand and remember the love and light that you felt, connecting you to everything else in the Universe. Take a deep breath and thank the beautiful ocean water for its healing power.

OUR WATER

All around, a cold, grey day
When does the big rain end?
Where does the sea go anyway?
Seems a puzzle to comprehend.

Rain columns come vertically down
Pounding, thunder, ejaculating,
Leaving seeds to be sown,
Green womb of Earth, expecting.

On a white and snowy day
Sparkling crystals swirl round.
A cloud of them—hard to say—
Still floating, or on the ground?

Rolling lands receive snow melting.
Warm, content, they hold semen lakes,
Birthing rivers across the meadows,
Fertile land, fields now awake.

Wondrous Mother receives the seeds,
Holding, nourishing, watching them grow.
Birthing abundance for our needs:
Cherries, berries, sweet miracles aglow.

Is there another drop to spare?
Or will more water always be there?

The Fairie Hill

While atop the Hollow Hill, near Lough Gur, Ireland, I had an experience that again took me into another dimension. The three of us who had trekked all the way up there to the summit, under the fences, and through the cow pasture, wandered around after we had finally arrived at the top of the Fairie Hill.

We were amazed to find a circle in the grass, a ceremonial footpath that had been formed from centuries of Celtic ceremonies at this hallowed site. We laid down along the perimeter of the circle at the very top of the hill and placed our heads on the sacred ground. It was peaceful, with the lake way below and a special quiet on the fabled hill where Celts had gathered throughout the eons.

I was on my back and watched a tiny bird begin to fly around us all by itself, singing as happily as could be. It continued circling with its cheerful song, its wings beating so quickly that I could hardly see them. Since it was as diminutive as any fairy might be, I felt it was a message from them, letting us know they were happy that we were there. I felt a great deal of joy lying on the soft grass. I looked up to see how my companions were doing. To my surprise, they were both lying on their stomachs, cheeks on the grass. "Well," I thought, "I'll try that, too."

The earth smelled rich like autumn leaves, well-cured manure, mushrooms, and Persian roses all tumbled together. I closed my eyes and the fragrance of the earth drew me in immediately. I found myself in a dark tunnel, going deep into Mother Earth. The smell became dank, almost moldy. But for whatever reason, I felt compelled to keep going down through the dark tunnel.

Soon, I arrived in a warm, golden, glowing cubicle room. A door closed behind me and there I was, alone—but not, really.

The Magic of the Real World

I realized that fluttering all about were hundreds of tiny, winged, golden, luminous beings. They reminded me of miniature dragonflies. They never stopped moving their wings, which were going at a rapid rate. The energy in the space was so very alive.

They seemed super excited that someone was actually in the room with them, but they never stopped to say hello; they were busily generating the golden light. The room itself seemed like an antechamber, like it was a waiting place in preparation for something special to happen, so I waited there, amazed at the high vibration in the golden light.

I wondered why it was such a precise cube. Looking up the walls, I saw that the room was windowless and the corners were perfectly measured, square upon square. The light inside was bright, warm, and golden, creating a sense of relaxing comfort. I was enchanted by it all, yet I continued to wonder why I could not create some sort of contact with the winged beings.

After a while, a previously unnoticed door on the other side opened into darkness. As my eyes began to focus, I was able to discern a forest in the distance and I approached the doorway, but looking out, I immediately missed the warmth and brightness of the antechamber. Curious, my eyes adjusted to the dark. I could see tall, slender white trees with leafy green branches out there. Then a tree that looked like a tall birch came to life by moving one of its leafy branches. I noticed its mouth, high up on the trunk. Then I heard it tell me to come closer. I stepped out of my golden warmth and into the cool forest.

The tree spirit said to me in a low, calm voice full of love, "I'm glad you have come." I felt like I was standing in front of the school principal—a little apprehensive, but ready. At the end of its long, branch arm was a rather heavy-looking crystal, shaped like a giant wand. The tree reached out and held the tip of that long crystal tenderly on the top of my head for what seemed like just the right amount of time. I felt an electric energy flow through me from my head down through my feet, anchoring into the ground beneath. The tree spirit waited silently for a while, holding the crystal with its long arm, then gently said, "Now, you must be going." I felt blessed, like I had received a very special benediction.

The Magic of the Real World

In an instant, I was back on the hilltop, lying in the grass, smelling the rich, sweet earth. I looked up and saw my friends still lying there around the circle on the Fairie Hill. Sitting up in the cool autumn air, the beautiful vision of the warm, golden, cubicle room all aflutter with energy was clearly alive in my mind. Had I been through a portal to the realms of the Tuatha De Danann, the ancient residents of Ireland who now live underground on the Emerald Island? As I waited for my friends, I contemplated this idea and was thrilled to think that I had visited with the Shining Ones.

Pondering Notes

This journey is clearly about the wise beings who live in the underworld here on Gaia. They want to connect with us, share blessings with us, and be a part of our lives. I have learned that shamanic journeys offer ways to connect with these special guides.

Cubes

Finding myself inside a beautiful, warm cubicle room deep within our Earth was a confirmation of the hexahedron shape that represents the earth element and our connection with life and nature. According to Plato, Earth is made of cubes, solid and firm, representing the experience of the concrete world. In sacred geometry, the patterning of the cube, such as Metatron's Cube, can transport a person to another place that can be considered zero point. Being in a cube like this helps us to feel the magic and intelligence of sacred geometry and assists our vibrational alignment process by weaving us together with the universe.

Golden Light

The golden light inside the wonderful cube holds the highest hertz/frequency that exists. Whatever is supposed to happen in this environment will happen. A stable environment filled with golden light will energize and heal us. The golden light enables transformation and immediate change. Like the sunlight, golden light heals the heart.

Insect Energy

Bees, dragonflies, butterflies, and other flying insects can generate warmth or coolness by using their wings. These busy little beings that I encountered were possibly solar fire angels. They were working hard to generate the warm, generous energy inside the cube. When the door opened into the cool darkness, I wanted to stay inside. However, when the tree spirit invited me to step out, I understood that it was an important step in continuing my journey. The tree put me at ease, and I found the courage to cross the portal, even though it was beyond my comfort zone. I was rewarded for my courage with a very special blessing from the tree spirit. I learned the important lesson of saying *yes* to new spiritual encounters that feel right.

Birch Trees

Birch trees are symbolic of hope, new beginnings and growth. The birch is a sacred tree among the Celts and has a protective influence. This tree supports childlike innocence and a resolve for adventure beyond the ordinary. It sparks new beginnings for body, mind, and soul. Spiritually, the birch represents nourishment, transformation, and liberation.

The essential power of the birch trees is to creatively bring dreams together and help us prepare for new patterns of living. Therefore, it comes as no surprise that the tree spirit was holding and blessing me with a magic crystal wand.

Crystal Wand

Crystal wands are healing tools that some say were used long ago in Lemuria and Atlantis. They tap into the energy of the universe and stimulate the human energy field. They are used for balancing, cleansing, protection, and spiritual development.

The blessing I received was like the shimmering energy of a waterfall, electrically charging me from head to toe. Of course, the crystal comes from the middle of the Earth and brings powerful healing and many other benefits. Some teachers instruct that we should each imagine ourselves inside a crystal for protection and healing.

When the tree spirit told me it was time to go, I left immediately. It is important to trust your guides and do as they say.

Tuatha De Danann

I wondered about a connection with the Tuatha De Danann because I was in Ireland, where the legendary entities are fabled to live underground in the Hollow Hills. They are an ancient, magical race of supernatural beings with marvelous powers and skills.

Stories of them are filled with legends of sacred oak trees, swords of light, and magical swans. They inhabited Ireland many eons ago but decided to go underground when they felt danger from intruders who came from another place. However, it is believed they still exist in Ireland underground, and they like to interact with humans.

Also known as the Sidhe, the Tuatha De Danann control the ripening of the crops and production of cows' milk. They are a part of modern-day Irish folklore, featuring fairies, gnomes, and elves. They never grow old because they live in Tir na nOg, the Land of the Young. We can reach the Tuatha De Danann, also known as the Shining People, through ancient underground caverns assumed to have been abandoned long ago. But for some of us, they are obviously still functional today.

Meditation with Mother Earth

> To access a video recording of the meditation, scan this code:

In this meditation, we will visit the womb of the primal great Mother, our Earth. Our Earth is amazing! It is our home and also home to all the waters, the winds and airs, trees, flowers and plants, animals, dolphins, minerals, crystals, all of us humans and it is the source of all our food. Spinning around in our universe, it supports all of this life. Our Mother Earth is constantly giving to us and providing everything we need to create wonderful, nurturing lives for ourselves throughout every cycle. As we stand on the Earth, we can think of ourselves as being planted here.

What is under our feet? In earthly terms, we can call the rich, dark soil "compost." This could be another word for transmutation. All of our power comes from the Earth. Our roots grow down into the soil, into the darkness…a darkness that nourishes us.

Remember that when we plant a seed, we plant it down in the dark soil, not in the light. It is there where seeds germinate and grow. After they bloom and celebrate in the light, they go back down into the soil again. This is where magic occurs in the unknown mystery. Some say it is where human souls become Human Beings. We will start our journey to visit the womb of our Earth Mother by entering into a dark cave on our beautiful planet.

Imagine that you are watching a lovely sunset. The sky is blazing orange and there are some threads of purple clouds on the horizon. You are standing at the edge of a cave with a large opening. It welcomes you to come inside. You step in, just at the entrance. You can see that it is a big cave that goes back a long way, so far that you cannot see the back of it. Turning around, you notice that the sun has now fallen below the horizon and the sky is getting darker. With the last of the daylight, you walk on into the cave, toward the back. You intend to develop a relationship with the Darkness of Underground. You have an understanding that this can bring stability in your life, by balancing your experience of the light with the dark. Walking on further, touching your hands against the wall to guide you, you sense a comfortable place to sit. Leaning against the wall of the cave, you sit down. Take a deep breath in and let it out into the darkness with a deep sigh.

What is present there with you? You listen for sounds. You can hear some drip, drip, dripping. You open your eyes wider to try to see more…but it is only blackness. You realize that it is time to focus on being strong and finding your courage in this darkness. Reaching your arms out, you hug the formless darkness. Why are you here? You begin to feel humbled by the vast darkness. You ask for help to release everything you do not want anymore, relieving your burden and making space for something new. Breathe a few deep breaths into your lungs. Now open your heart space for some kind of message. (Remember that we can create from the invisible…so you expect to receive a message.) And you will receive a message from the darkness. It might be some meaningful words, a solution to something you have been pondering, or a sense of knowing. Take some time to receive this important message. What is the gift you are receiving?

As you are sitting there, feeling enveloped by the darkness, something begins to shift. Towards the back of the cave, a light begins to form in a misty veil. The energy in the light grows brighter and begins to shimmer with radiance. It beckons to you. As you recall that the greatest light shines forth from the deepest darkness, you stand at attention. From your stance, you see a pathway to the new light at the very back of the cave, and you walk toward it. Now that you are there, you see an illuminated tunnel of light shining downward. You enter this tunnel and begin your descent down. There are no steps, you simply float downward.

The walls of this tunnel are made of golden obsidian mirrors and they glow with a luminescent light. You follow the tunnel for a while as it spirals around and continues down. You are feeling purified by the golden obsidian, which you are passing through. Old damaging memories are being erased. Take a moment to enjoy this cleansing and the relief it brings. You feel a renewed sense of peace and balance.

After a while, you descend into a large, open room inside a vast crystal cathedral. Immediately you hear the song you know from the ancient language of Light. All your senses are attuned to the source of the magical sound.

Then you see her, the ancient Grandmother who is creating all new things from the middle of the Earth, throughout all cycles of time. Everything around this beautiful Being is sparkling and vibrant with tall crystals of all colors. It is spectacular there and full of welcoming love. Grandmother walks toward you and gives you a warm embrace. She knows who you are. You feel your heart melting with gratefulness and happiness. She invites you to sit down next to her. You spend some time, silently connecting your hearts. She has chosen to meet you. Notice everything about her. Take some deep breaths and appreciate this opportunity to be within the love of the Grandmother.

You ask her what you can offer her. She begins to teach you as if to say that when you understand and apply her teachings, that will be sufficient. That would please her. "Look around," she says. "Do you see all these brilliant, sparkling crystals? Every person on earth is a crystal, just like these. As humans work on themselves by following some advice that I will offer you, they will gradually polish up their crystalline nature from a stone into a sparkling crystal."

She asks you which sparkling color of crystal are you becoming.

Grandmother begins to share advice for you. "Do not give any more power to sadness, because today you need to live and be happy. To continue on the surface of Mother Earth, you need to love your life." Grandmother goes on to explain that you came to Earth prepared for any challenge and that the Creator gave you what you need to be well and happy, although perhaps not always what you may have wanted.

"Humans are still in a growth process," she says. "Especially now, your Earth needs a loving touch and kind words from you. Just like a child or friend, Earth is filled with happiness from your love." Grandmother tells you to allow yourself to touch the world with all of who you are. Healing exists all around…you just need to connect with it.

After a pause, Grandmother continues with more important teachings. She says it is essential to let go of negative energies since they not only affect you but also many others around you.

"Be sure to let go of all that. No one needs to be hurt. You have control over your own well-being; nobody can hurt you. Believe that you are a good Human Being. You are a crystal and a crystal is a Light."

She ends the teaching by telling you that when you say prayers, thousands of Beings throughout the Earth and the Galaxies are listening to you.

You had asked her what you could offer her, and she has given you many gift ideas to focus on. As you gaze at her, you see that she is enveloped in a misty glow of rosy light. She has a crystal wand in her hand. She stands and touches your head with it. The energy comes through your body like lightning. The power and electricity of it is jolting. It feels like a wake-up call.

After some moments, you understand that it is time for you to go. You thank Grandmother Earth from the bottom of your heart for all her teachings and blessings. You promise to do your best with all the advice of lovingness that she has given you in the Crystal Cathedral.

Suddenly, you are caught up in a swirling mist of white light and you find yourself spiraling back up the obsidian tunnel to the cave. Stepping onto the ground in the cave, you look out through the entrance and see the light of dawn. You walk out of the cave entrance and greet the rising Sun.

Standing there feeling connected to the Earth, you revel in the warmth, power, beauty, and the new day of Father Sun. Mother Earth's teachings are fresh in your memory and, feeling filled with love as a Mother has for a child, you bend down to kiss the Earth.

Dancing Trees, Transfiguring

Some hum mantras with the bees,
Or bow, when birds on them alight.
Dancing gently in a soft breeze,
Yet in strong winds they swing with might.

I wonder what the tree beings sing
When they send their roots to reach
Into the heart of Mother, mingling,
Giving, receiving, always to teach.

When rains come to quench their thirst
Graceful, meandering waters lap sweet
Through branches, roots, leaves, at first
Blessing the sky with prayers, complete.

What happens when hot fires burn
Changing the blazing forests to black?
They celebrate with a bright gold turn,
Dissolve to ash, they will come back.

In Balance with Sekhmet

On a tour of Egypt, a small group of us arrived at the Temple of Ptah at the great site of Karnak, the ancient "Chamber of the Heart." We intended to visit the tall black granite statue of Sekhmet inside the little room where she has stood in the same place, unmoved for centuries.

There are many names for Sekhmet: Lady of Transformation, Lady of Enchantment, Opener of Ways, and Great One of Healing. We were excited for this encounter. With two groups of people waiting to go inside for private ceremonies, we slipped in before they became organized. Quickly, we set up an altar and took out our crystals and other ceremonial objects so that we could honor Sekhmet. We each settled on a place that was as comfortable as we could make it. It was a tight fit, as an archaeological team was working on the building, and it felt almost as if we were in a construction zone, cramped in the room.

We received instructions from our group leader to open up our hearts for Sekhmet, the infamous Egyptian Goddess, so we toned her name and called in her essence through chanting. Then we heard the lapis crystal bowl played by the leader of our small group. As I sat there, I thought about opening my heart for Sekhmet, something that I wanted to do. The large crystal lotus flower that exists in my heart chakra began to form. In the center of the flower is a small space, the kind you might see in the middle of a spiral. Before I knew it, as my heart opened wide, in jumped Sekhmet, like a lion leaping through a hoop. There she was, looking out of the window in my heart.

I was mesmerized by the depth of her eyes, which gazed right through me and clearly saw everything about me. She began to tell me about herself—that she was gentle and a nurturing, loving mother being, who was healing and helpful. However, she was also strong and could at any time stand alone. She was quite capable of taking care of herself against all odds, even able to fight off violent enemies. The key, she explained, was to keep the two traits in perfect balance.

She told me to listen. I felt that I had the ears of a lion now and I began to listen to the toning of the crystal bowl. At first, I only heard it in one ear, then the other ear. She told me this was not in balance. I needed to be able to hear the sound evenly in both ears, as only that would bring balance. This took a concentrated effort. She explained that this was how to keep the qualities of gentleness and strength in balance: through careful consideration, concentration, and a striving for purpose. It was not easy to get the toning of that crystal bowl to be even in both ears. It rang louder in one ear, then in the other. It took work to be able to hear the toning equally in both ears at the same time. Finally, I got it.

Once the sound was equally balanced in both my ears, Sekhmet explained that now I was ready for more teaching. She led me out into the jungle to give me another lesson in balance. We went along a jungle pathway to a river. Walking along the muddy bank, we saw vines, fallen trees, and murky waters. It felt dark and scary because I didn't know what was lurking back in the jungle. But I followed Sekhmet. Intuitively, I knew I had agreed to this lesson and trusted her as my guide.

Suddenly, she powerfully jumped up, in her agile, cat-like way, to a tree trunk that had fallen and crossed the river. It was perched high up, supported by both banks, and held fast directly over a swirling, foaming pool of water. Then she gracefully began to follow the top line of the log, placing one paw silently in front of the other, so that her four paws were carefully placed in one single line along the log. In this way, she was crossing the river. I was mesmerized by the movement of her graceful golden body. When she got to the middle, she stopped and looked back at me, waiting. I knew this meant it was my turn to climb up from the bank and find my way along the narrow log over the angry waters below.

I climbed up but I hesitated. How would I get across? One foot first, softly, just like she did it. I kept my center of gravity on the foot that was planted there, while I moved the other around in front, in a way that kept me from leaning too far right or too far left. Arms out, I stayed in balance. I focused and did not think about the roiling river below me. I took my time, going slowly and with purpose. I looked up in front of me and there she was, pulling me along with her powerful eyes. I knew I could do this.

In Balance with Sekhmet

The next group was coming into the temple now, which disturbed our meditation, so my journey with Sekhmet stopped there, temporarily. I was sad but grateful that we had gone so far together.

I have thought about this story many times and envisioned a new ending with Sekhmet because I felt the story was incomplete. I share the next part of the story here with you.

I know that Sekhmet wanted me to see how powerful she was so that I could comprehend how she could be both a gentle teacher and a strong defender, living a life in balance. She had already shown me the gentle teacher aspect.

Getting to the other side of the river was a boost to my sense of worthiness. I felt more confident as she led me along a trail through the jungle.

After a while, the trail broke into the open. Grasslands were visible for miles and we continued along the river, now walking through the tall grasses. Suddenly, I saw her freeze. She was looking toward the river. I followed her gaze and then I heard the growling. There was another lioness caught in the grip of a crocodile.

Sekhmet lunged forward and was at the scene in seconds. She tore at the tail of the huge crocodile, but it had the leg of the lioness caught in its jaws. Sekhmet knew what to do. She fearlessly threw herself in front of the crocodile, grabbed the upper jaw of the big animal, and ripped it off the lioness. Then she tore the crocodile apart.

It was like a war zone with all the blood and loud noises exploding everywhere. After a while, the crocodile lay there in pieces. The wounded lioness lay there, too, but she was still intact. Her leg looked bloody but not broken. Sekhmet had made it just in time.

Sekhmet stood over the other lioness, licking her wounds and caring for her. It was an act of pure heroism. She lay down next to her hurt friend. I waited, afraid to get too close to the scene. Finally, she looked up at me. Her fantastic, glowing eyes gave me the message: now it was my turn to be brave. I would have to go back by myself, without her trusted guidance, over the boiling river, and through the scary jungle. This would be a true initiation for me.

In Balance with Sekhmet

Sekhmet had taught me the lessons I needed to learn about how to trust myself to make it on my own. I knew that I would be both strong and gentle: listening, confronting my fears while going over the river, passing through the dark jungle, and taking action for myself. This effort exemplifies the alchemical fire of transmutation. I feel grateful for the opportunity to have achieved this empowered state of grace on my journey with Sekhmet.

Pondering Notes

Sekhmet, Lioness

When a lion shows up in our dreams, it is a sign for us to step into our birthright of power; we are each born powerful and divine. The feeling that I received from Sekhmet was that she was a queen, full of authority, sovereign integrity, and power. This is characteristic of the lion family.

In fact, Sekhmet is one of the most famous Egyptian deities and her name can be translated as "the Powerful One." She is depicted as a woman with the head of a lioness. In ancient Egypt, she was known for her destructive powers and led the pharaohs in warfare. However, she was also well known for her healing and protective powers.

I was pleased to meet Sekhmet in my own heart space because it allowed me to embrace her as an ally. This provided me the opportunity to self-initiate a pathway to become more powerful myself. Sekhmet is the perfect teacher regarding balance because her character contains both the aspects of a ravaging warrior, fighting for what is right, and a powerful healer, bringing peace. This combination can be a part of all of us. Actually, it is a part of the entire cosmos.

Lion's beautiful eyes are translucent, like crystals. They are entrances to the hidden void, an invitation to contemplate the mysteries of creation. Sekhmet's eyes had the power to guide me, pull me, and give me messages.

Crocodiles

In ancient Egypt, crocodiles were both feared and loved. They were feared because they are aggressive, violent, unpredictable, and extremely powerful. They were also revered because they were thought to protect the innocent and bring new sight to the dead.

Today, crocodiles can represent archaic ways of seeing, the ancient aspects that keep us trapped and try to destroy us. Their energy has been linked to dragon energy, which has been misrepresented in popular culture as power at its worst and equal to the worst of what humans can become. This association would make it difficult for us to come to terms with our real power, which is actually filled with Light.

However, a new definition of dragon energy is emerging. With the evolution of our changing consciousness, many are finding dragon companions along their paths. The reports are that these are magical, high-frequency beings and that dragons and their healing powers are electromagnetic, multidimensional, and beautiful to work with. These dragons can help people learn how to expand their Inner Light, their Healing Powers, and their very own Magic.

Balance

Finding balance in life seems like an ongoing endeavor. However, especially in today's fast-paced, modern world, maintaining a balanced life is essential for health, peace of mind, and well-being. Balance requires discipline and concentration to accomplish our responsibilities. Balance comes from an inward drive. It is important for us to take time to do things that fill our souls with happiness. Life does not need to be hard. It all depends on our perception.

Balance means embracing the light and the dark. It equals the capacity to self-regulate and adapt. When we can give unconditional love with protective boundaries, not expecting anything in return, then we can find pure joy in existence.

Thank you, Sekhmet, for these invaluable insights.

Meditation with Sekhmet

> To access a video recording of the meditation, scan this code:

In this meditation, we will visit Sekhmet, the Egyptian Goddess who has the head of a lioness and the body of a woman. There are many feline power animals around the world. For example, the Maya believe that the jaguar is the symbol of life and strength, the gatekeeper to everything unknown that can provide us with the power to face our fears. The puma in the Andes is similarly held with an appreciation of its great powers.

Goddess Sekhmet carries a combination of destructive and creative forces, yielding both dichotomy and complexity in her being. Along with all cats, she embodies the energy of fire. But hers is especially powerful since she was created from the fire in the eye of Ra, the God of the Sun. Sekhmet is pictured with the following symbols: the Solar Disk, which represents the giver of light, warmth, and life to our Earth, together with the Uraeno (striking cobra), indicating divine authority; the Ankh, representing eternal life, and the Staff, which is the scepter of power. Therefore, it is not surprising that Sekhmet is known by some of the following names: the Powerful Female One, the Scarlet Lady, and the Avenger of Wrongs.

In mythical history, Sekhmet was a fierce warrior Goddess who could bring death, fear, destruction, and suffering, thereby representing ancient human fears that continue to affect people and our world today. In contrast, she was also known as the Goddess of Healing, Love, Peace, and Protection. Her priests were doctors and she could protect all the people as if they were her baby cubs.

Soon, when we encounter Sekhmet in the sun-baked desert sands, we will ask her for help from both sides of her personality: the side that destroys things that do not serve us in the fires of transformation and also the gentle, healing, and compassionate side, full of Love, providing qualities that we need now. Sekhmet has the characteristic of showing up when we need her. She works with our energy and our requirements for the highest good of all.

Now we will start our meditation:

Quiet your mind as you let go of the daily chatter; focus on your breath rising and falling through your body. Gently place a hand on your heart as you continue to settle into the presence of your breath as it flows, going deeper and deeper through your body, within the landscape of your soul.

As you do this, you begin to feel or see a door in your heart and with each breath, it opens a little wider. You can feel the warmth of the sun shining in. You step out of the door and find that you are standing on the hot desert sand. You feel the heat on the bottoms of your feet and look up at the brilliant blue sky with the golden sun blazing down. In the distance, you can see a river flowing and beyond that, pyramids. The warmth and light of the sun melt away any worry or fear about where you are. You feel safe and protected in the warm, fragrant desert air. Take a few deep breaths in and out.

You understand that you are now in the land of Sekhmet. The Lady of the Flames has the power to transmute dark feelings into the highest vibration of pure unconditional love. You call on her now to help you destroy anything that is preventing you from being in your highest vibration. As you walk along, the hot sand is almost burning the bottoms of your feet. You would like to cool them off in the river water. But you are comfortable enough and feel good in the warm light of the sun.

Suddenly, you hear a loud roar, echoing throughout the desert. It is coming from the direction of the sun. Turning toward that direction, you squint to see what could be making such an explosive, reverberating sound. Then you see her, coming from the sun toward you. It is Sekhmet herself, in a long, red dress, the golden solar disk on her lion head shining forth. There are flames surrounding her form as she comes your way, directly out of the silhouette of the sun. You stop and watch as she travels in flaming red and golden light towards you.

You pray, "Goddess, help me. I offer you my heart, my own inner sun. Please help me with any problems that need to be healed." You call in all your angels and guides to be there with you, to protect you. Ask to be filled with light, with whatever you need to be strong enough to greet her.

You feel the hot desert winds stirring around you as she approaches. She is walking along the sand toward you now. As you wait to see what will happen, you realize that you must be strong. She approaches you and you focus on one thing—the golden light streaming out of her eyes.

You draw that liquid golden light into your own eyes. Allow it to fill your head. Now it spreads down your neck, across your shoulders, down your arms, into your hands. The golden light flows down into your chest, it fills your heart, and continues to fill up your belly and down past your hips, into your legs and your feet. As Sekhmet's golden light flows throughout your body, it washes away your pains, anger, doubts, worry, judgments, sadness, weariness, and all your fears. Let that golden light work on your essential being for as long as you need it to. Her golden light is absorbing all these harmful energies and transmuting them.

When you are ready, look into her eyes again and let the golden liquid flow back into her.

Now notice inside of yourself that you feel beautiful, clean, open, aware, expansive, happy, and connected to the Divine. You become aware that standing quietly by your side is this same golden lioness woman, a divine being invited to be with you now as you journey even deeper into your inner awareness. You can feel the tenderness and love flowing from her whole being.

You become aware that surrounding you both is a choir of white angels. There are hundreds of angels in the vast desert air, all gently moving their wings and fanning you, keeping you cool and comfortable. You receive a blessing from them. In the message, you understand that the angels are working together with Sekhmet to help heal the Earth at this time. Furthermore, you hear that this must start with each individual who is alive now. It is time to walk along your path with beauty.

Sekhmet will accompany you as a protector of your heart and give you courage for the quest that you are on. You are asking on this inner quest to have a question answered, a way shown, to receive a gift, so that you can contribute your part to this evolutionary work.

As you walk with Sekhmet, the Goddess of Power, Strength, Love and Courage, you are safe and protected. Sekhmet is with you to tenderly guide you to the answer that will allow you to have more peace and balance in your life and to reach an empowered state of grace, to help you walk on your trail of beauty. Breathe with her and be with her now as she takes you on a journey of more awareness, knowledge, and love.

Take some time to experience what Sekhmet is showing you.

When you are ready, allow yourself to gather up the love, the ideas, and the messages that were shown to you by Sekhmet and put these into a safe place to be used again and again.

Beginning your journey back, Sekhmet and the angels continue to go along with you until you are back to this time and space and place. You thank them all for everything with your heart full of reverence and love.

Breathing gently, you feel the warmth of sunlight flowing in your body, the strength and courage of Sekhmet pulsing in your heart, the love of the angels surrounding you. You know that wherever you are, wherever you go, you will have the power, courage, and gentle nurturing of these divine helpers with you.

The lovely choir of angels slowly begins to dissolve from your sight and you find yourself back where you began.

I will say the Beauty Prayer for you now:

A Navajo/Dine´ Prayer

In beauty may I walk
All day long may I walk
Through the returning seasons may I walk
Beautifully will I possess again
Beautifully birds,
Beautifully joyful birds
On the trail marked with pollen may I walk
With grasshoppers about my feet may I walk
With dew about my feet may I walk
With beauty may I walk
With beauty before me may I walk
With beauty behind me may I walk
With beauty above me may I walk
With beauty all around me may I walk
In old age, wandering on a trail of beauty, lively, may I walk
In old age, wandering on a trail of beauty, living again, may I walk
It is finished in beauty.
It is finished in beauty.

FIRE LOVER

The fire seduced me tonight.
Orange flames licking my soul
Warmed with happiness, filled with delight.

Breezes blow, igniting the coals.
Mysteries of dark and light
So visible, caught in the fire's glow.

As air starts to cool, we embrace
Close together, alive and hopeful,
Sun setting, the day's final grace.

Firekeeper adds more wood.
Welcoming, it leaps higher.
Now the singing, assured and good.

Chants circling around the fire.
I am back with my ancestors.
Drums, songs, prayers inspire.

Precious memories for us today.
Returning to the distant stars,
Following along the Milky Way.

Coming back, through the Black
With my love, the blazing fire—
Home again, welcome back.

WHAT IS ABU GHURAB?

A date-palmed path wound through a poor Egyptian village and out into the desert. When we got to the end of the trail, the desert opened up before us. We saw a pyramid in ruins, surrounded by blowing sand. In the area were the remains of some large, round basins. We wandered about with a great sense of curiosity. The basins were highly polished alabaster pieces.

Inspecting these heavy, round remains that had been created in a long-bygone era triggered musings of a sophisticated ancient technology. Could these crystalline stones have been created by a type of advanced machine work in order to make their smooth and perfectly circular shapes? This was an interesting question.

However, even more intriguing was a large, shining mandala-shaped altar perched next to the dilapidated pyramid. It was the most prominent aspect of this place. It was made of pure travertine, a rare stone in Egypt. The altar was constructed of six pieces with points to the four directions and it was glittering with crystals.

There is some consensus among archaeologists that in ancient times, the round center of the mandala held an obelisk that rose as high as 50 meters and had a traditional conical metal top, used as a conductor of some sort. (This was apparently common in ancient Egypt.) It could have been a Hotep, which hieroglyphs describe as "an altar". Interestingly, the word "hotep" from ancient Egyptian means "to be at peace." The altar was perfectly aligned, North to South and East to West.

A small group of us arrived at Abu Ghurab on November 11, 2011: 11/11/11. It was a day that carried many of the ancient Egyptian goddess Hathor's qualities because of the astronomical alignments with Venus, who represents the essence of beauty, love, and divine feminine energy.

Not many people come to visit this place in Egypt. A little group of local children followed us up through the date palms into the area. They wanted pens and pencils so they could draw and write. After talking with them and enjoying their beautiful faces, we handed out pens and pencils. Then we prepared for our work. Our small group set about to meditate on the mandala-shaped altar which rose above the ground about five feet. Each of us climbed up there and found a spot, settling as comfortably as we could onto the hard crystalline structure.

What is special about this place is that, while sitting outside in the desert sun, one can gaze at magnificent views of the Giza Plateau to the north and the three prominent but lesser-known pyramids to the south. From where we were sitting on the mandala, we could also see the now-crumbling pyramid to the west that had been constructed there eons ago (some say at least 12,000 years ago). To the east was the Nile River.

With all these wonders around us and the dry, fragrant desert air, it was easy to begin our meditation. As I deepened into it, I traveled in my mind to the place where I often meet my guides. I went trekking down an imaginary set of stairs and headed out to my own cherished desert. This is my sanctuary place where I know that I can safely trust my guides. They were there, reliably waiting for me. They helped me get onto my healing table at the edge of a little ravine, deep in the red rocks.

As usual, at my left shoulder was my beautiful, tall white angel and to my right, my Native American guide. At my left foot was the Ascended Master Kuthumi, and the Goddess Isis showed up by my right foot. Those were my four guides for this time, as I lay on my healing table wondering what would happen. I felt excited and totally supported.

It was not long before I left my body. My spirit levitated above the table. Without speaking, the guides assured me that all was well and that they would stay with me. Next, they gently arranged my limbs so that I was a five-pointed star, like the many stars I had seen painted on the ceilings of the ancient temples along the Nile: two legs, pulled apart, two arms stretched out, with my head as the fifth point.

As I was already floating with the help of my guides, I felt myself journeying higher and higher up. Soon, I was turning head over heels in this position, then spinning through space in an elliptical orbit. Up and out I went. This continued for a long time until I was deep into the starry universe. Then, finally, I found I had traveled all the way to the Pleiades. There I stopped, face-to-face with the goddess Hathor herself.

What Is Abu Ghurab?

She was beautiful, bathed in pink light with the most loving face and kind, gentle eyes. She blessed me with her gaze and I knew this was my opportunity to ask her for help, so I did ask for help: good health, strength, kindness, wisdom, and happiness. To my surprise, she asked me why I wanted these qualities. I paused for some time and got my thoughts in order until I told her I wanted to have these qualities so I could help others—my family, friends, community, and our world—in the best ways possible.

I felt that it would be advantageous to embrace these qualities for that sense of social responsibility that we are all feeling now. After my answer, she blessed me again. She told me that because of the reasons I gave her, she would help me. I felt so humbled by her precious blessing. She was so beautiful in every way. All I could do was thank her for everything.

As I spun back into my star shape and headed back to Earth, I halted for a while because I had a vision of millions of people who were all looking in one direction.

All I saw were their faces as they gazed toward a bright light that was reflected in their eyes. It occurred to me that this could be the world population, coming together for the new civilization, the Newness Time, embraced by the divine feminine nature. Could there be a time coming when the entire human species would incarnate as a single being…with a consciousness that integrates all our lifestyles and adventures, yielding a single consciousness?

Continuing on my journey, I saw a gigantic black hole far away in the distance. Flowing through it was a gaseous material full of millions of tiny crystals, each emanating a prismatic, colorful light. There was something strange about it because everything was flowing backwards. It appeared like a self-contained reversed fountain but instead of water, it was full of sparkling, tiny crystals, like an amazing upside-down fireworks display. I watched this fantastic movement perpetuate itself. The colors were mesmerizing—electric pink, green, purple, blue, gold, and a brilliant white.

What Is Abu Ghurab?

127

The Magic of the Real World

Then something changed. The little crystals collected themselves into one gigantic crystal. The spinning from the middle of the black hole forced the new gigantic crystal to become suspended directly above the middle of the black hole. There was the solitary crystal on an energetic plane of its own. Now it was simply spinning with an array of brilliant, refracted colors above the middle of the black hole and flashing out amazing lights, like the beacons of thousands of lighthouses.

This display continued for a long time, at least as long as I was watching. I was completely hypnotized by the beautiful spectacle of color and light. It seemed like energetic scalar waves were being distributed throughout the universe for the good and healing of all things. I gazed at the spectacle for quite a while, trying to comprehend all the workings and the effects of what I was witnessing.

Suddenly, I was returned back to my healing table. What a journey! I thanked each of my guides, then got down and walked back along the path. I stomped my feet up the steps, grounding myself as I went back up out of my red rock garden, past the trees and flowers, and home again—to the present moment.

Looking back, it is hard not to wonder about the energies of the day, 11/11/2011, and also what took place at the Sun Temple at Abu Ghurab so many centuries ago. It certainly is a place with special powers, but what exactly did the ancients do there? This remains a mystery.

Pondering Notes

Abu Ghurab

Abu Ghurab is a location that is a transmitter of energies from inside Gaia (our Earth) out to the universe. Goddess Hathor tends to this special place in Egypt. With the help of my guides, I was able to tune into the energy there. No one today seems to know when it was constructed, why, or how.

Number Five

Five-pointed stars have been found on Egyptian tombs and temples throughout the history of the ancient civilization. They represent destiny and are described as the homes of the successfully departed souls. Five (5) is a combination of two (2), the female energy, and three (3), the masculine energy, and subsequently, when combined, produce the "music of the spheres." An example of this is when Isis (2) and Osiris (3) produced Horus with their heavenly marriage. In ancient Egypt, five was considered the building block of the creation process.

Five is also found proliferating in the most beautiful ways throughout nature. One can detect the number five in roses, flowers, apples, and other fruits. When observed from Earth, Venus, a planet and deity associated with the Goddess Hathor, creates a five-pointed pattern during her orbit together with the Sun around our Earth. There are also five elements: ether, air, fire, water, and earth, that are simultaneously present within each one of us.

Pleiades

Hathor is a goddess from the Pleiades. She represents essential love, pink healing light, and happiness. The Pleiades is a group of stars that we can see from Earth at certain times of the year. When we look at this group of stars, they often seem to be pulsating. That is because they are alive. So many civilizations claim to have originated in the Pleiades—27 different ones on Earth starting with Atlantis and moving on to the Egyptian, Maya, Incan, Lakota, Cherokee, Hawaiian and numerous others. The Pleiades Cluster is a very powerful anchor of our earthly civilizations.

Goddess Hathor

Hathor is multifaceted in that she is a wife, mother, lover, and protector of women and children. It was a joy to connect with her and to receive her blessings. It is important to remember that when we go through a portal as I did while traveling to Hathor, if we meet a special being like she is, we should ask for something. Receiving it brings a sense of completeness. I felt so blessed and happy to receive my gifts.

Connecting to the One

The eyes of humanity reflecting one light is a compelling illustration that we all feel the connection to the One. This could be the One Sun, the light that we all come from, the Christ consciousness, or the light connected to whatever spirituality we work with. We can imagine that we are all roots of the same tree. As we come into what many spiritual leaders are calling a new era based on the energy of the divine feminine, it is a good thing for us to recognize the essential importance of this powerful, bright light of Oneness.

Black Holes

The black hole could represent the sacred womb space of all creation. Remember that darkness has light in it, and from light comes new life. A magnetic energy emanates from the activity within the black hole. The colors remind me of a kaleidoscope, where changing beams of energy come forth like scalar light waves full of iridescent rays.

Scalar waves are similar to powerful prayers. They travel faster than the speed of light; they seem to transcend space and time; they cause the molecular structure of water to become coherently reordered; they positively increase immune function in mammals, and they are involved in the formation process of all of nature. We can call on scalar waves at any time to help us with healing. This journey showed me that there is so much possibility coming forward. We have much potential to build from.

Guides

We all have guides who are just waiting for us to call on them. They want to help us. They can be angels, our ancestors, or other beloved entities. Please do call on these spirit guides to help because it will be beneficial for us all.

My Guides in This Story

Kuthumi: I connected with this man a long time ago. I had no idea who he was, but I had a distinct picture of him in my mind, especially his beautiful blue eyes and his white tunic. I had thought that perhaps he was Jesus, but truly I did not know who he was. He always showed up to lovingly support me with my prayers and journeys. One day I found his picture in a shop and could hardly believe that I was seeing him there. The name on the picture was Kuthumi. After researching him, I discovered that he is a revered Ascended Master. According to some sources, Kuthumi has been a previous Chohan of the Second Ray (meaning that he works with people defining the Yellow Ray of Illumination, helping to manifest wisdom, perception, joy, and lightness of being). Furthermore, according to some sources, he was St. Francis of Assisi in a past life and one of the three wise men, Balthazar.

Native American Guide: I have been blessed to have worked during my life with a powerful Lakota Medicine Woman who has since passed on to the spirit world. However, before she left, she explained to me that she is my Cola, which means she is my friend and spirit helper and is always available to guide me in my life. While explaining this, she asked me to pray for her family. And so I do that, to this day.

Angel: This beautiful, sweet angel was brought to my attention by a wonderful teacher and has stayed with me for many years. She is pure white and very tall, always showing up behind my left shoulder like she is connected to my heart.

Isis: She was a guide for me while I was in Egypt. Isis is a powerful goddess who may also have been Mary, the mother of Jesus. Both knew the feminine art of divine conception, whereby they could create new life within their wombs using their own creative life force energy. As a result, they both birthed avatars (incarnate divine teachers) named Jesus and Horus. There are other women, some even alive today, who have this capacity to generate erotic energy and create life within their own wombs, often birthing powerful teachers for humanity.

Meditation with the Pleiades

> To access a video recording of the meditation, scan this code:

In this meditation, we will journey to the Pleiades, a cluster of seven stars that seems to pulsate with light and energy in the night skies. Most indigenous cultures agree that we have a connection with the stars and many believe that the connection is especially strong with the Pleiades cluster. The Pleiades is a place of magical wonder deeply connected to our planet. There is a belief that the Pleiadians were instrumental in creating various civilizations around our Earth.

We will arrive at the Pleiades by way of an astral journey, flying past many stars out in the universe. Once we arrive there, we will have an interaction with Hathor, known as the Mother of the Cosmos. Hathor is said to reside in the Pleiades along with her six sisters. She is the beautiful Egyptian Goddess of love, healing, emotions, and music. This Mistress of Heaven represents our relationship to healing sound vibration and the harmonics of creation.

Let's start the meditation now.

Take a deep breath in through your crown chakra at the top of your head. From there, bring your breath down slowly into your heart center, and hold it there for a few seconds. Let your breath out with an "AH" through your mouth. This "AH" is the sound of the heart chakra. Take this breath one more time. On the third time, as you inhale through your crown chakra, bring a spark of light through the top of your head and pull it down along with your breath past your third eye, your throat chakra, and down into your heart space. Let it twinkle there in your heart space. Keep the spark of light there in your heart as you let your breath out with another "AHHH." Just rest with this light in your heart and feel happy. Put your hands over your heart and take another deep breath.

The crystal light that is twinkling in your heart wakes you up and draws you like a magnet through the dark, warm night air, attracting you to see some distant sparkling lights that are set out ahead of you. You can see past a grove of shadowy trees that the twinkling lights seem to be laid out like lanterns on the Earth in the distance. As you walk toward these lights, you begin to hear the ethereal vibrational sound of unseen crystal bowls. You put your hands to your heart to make sure that the light you brought inside with you is still there. You can feel that it is there and the light is getting bigger. Take another deep breath, letting it out with an "AHHH." You look up at the dark night sky and see that the stars are sparkling up there, similar to the lights that seem to be sparkling on the Earth in the distance, out in front of you. You remember the ancient teaching: As above, so below.

With wonder, you continue along your way toward the sparkling lights ahead. The pure tones of the crystal bowls fill you with a beautiful resonance. You are walking through the forest of trees now. Their grounding presence reassures you that all is well. Keeping your eyes on the lights before you, you continue walking, feeling your magnetic attraction toward them. Soon, you break through the forest of trees. A beautiful dark emerald meadow opens up in front of you. There you see a magnificent scene. Laid out in a perfect geometrical form is a large, seven-pointed star made of sparkling, shining crystalline lights. At the tippy points of each star ray is a special blue light—seven blue lights. The harmonic sounds create a high pulsating vibration in your ears. This is truly a magical meadow. As you gaze at the beautiful presentation of energy and light, you see in the middle center of the star, a small circle of blue light begins to pulsate. It beckons to you. You can feel the magnetic energy, inviting you to step into the form of the star, and on into the middle with the pulsating circle of blue light.

Take a deep breath before you venture forth. Inhale through your crown chakra. Slowly bring the energy down through your third eye…down through your throat chakra and into your heart space. Relax…everything is going well. You can feel the light there in your heart has grown so big that it fills your entire chest with beautiful sparkling crystalline white energy. Take another deep breath and relax. As your entire being is filled with a healing vibration, you meld into the energy of the twinkling lights before you.

You feel guided to step into the beautiful sparkling star, so you step in there and walk straight to the circle of blue light in the middle. You stand there just waiting, feeling safe and secure. You reach upward with your arms and look up with your face. There, you see the brilliant stars again, shining down at you. As you look up, you see a faint blue stream of light coming down to greet you. It comes closer and gets to be a stronger force of blue. Soon, you feel a connection with this tube of blue light that is reaching for you; it pulls at you. You want to go, but before you do so, you connect to Mother Earth, deep down into her roots. You give thanks to Mother Earth for all the life she gives to you. Then without resistance, you let go; you go with the pull of the blue stream of light and you rise up above the Earth. Spiraling, you are flying out into the cosmos, streaming past an ocean of stars, spinning in and out of a swirl of white and blue light and on out into the vast spaces. You slowly come to rest in a misty blue cloud. It is beautiful there and as you look around, you recognize the seven stars of the Pleiades that you have seen so many times from planet Earth.

As you adjust to the beautiful blue light and the brilliant stars, you can hear once more the magical vibration of ethereal sounds. It lifts your heart with happiness. The seven stars of the Pleiades form a circle around you as if to greet you in a special way. They are surrounding you with strength, confidence, trust and love that you can feel. Not knowing exactly what to do, you bow to each of the seven beautiful beings. You can feel a wonderful healing vibration coming into you from all sides. It is warm and seems to penetrate your very soul. You realize that you are in perfect harmony with these bright, loving star beings.

After a while, one of the seven stars steps up to greet you. She is surrounded by an aura of pink mist and she has a crown of horns with a sun in the middle of it. Also, she has cow ears. You recognize her immediately as Hathor herself, the Mother who provides nourishing milk for all humanity, the Lady of the Stars and the Goddess of Love. She steps closer and gives you an endearing hug. One of her star sisters comes forward with a small pink rose petal filled with honey. She tells you that the honey offering comes from the bees who come from the Great Sun and that honey gives you light and protects you from harm. You are grateful for the gift because you know that everyone needs light and protection. You put the rose petal filled with honey into your mouth and the sweetness of it ignites your entire being. You feel radiant happiness and Oneness with all of divine creation.

Hathor is standing in front of you, face to face. She says that she has a transmission for you.

You ask, "What do you want me to learn? I am open to your help."

Before she begins to speak, you hear the strands of her voice that she has wrapped within each star, beginning a dance of life with sounds of laughter and joy. The music of the spheres intensifies. You feel it permeating your whole being as if it is preparing your molecular structure more fully to receive her wisdom.

She begins to transmit:

You are a hero and we need your help. We are all part of a field of energy and each one of us can make a profound impact on this field. It is important to understand that our existence is simple. We can choose to live in fear, lack and chaos or in love, abundance, and happiness. When we choose to live in love, we positively impact the unified field. It only takes a few of us to change the energy of this field. It is our mission to raise the consciousness of those who are currently living on Earth and learning so many things right now. So how do we do this? Please listen to our words of love for you.

When there is low energy, remember to laugh and smile much more often. Think thoughts that are loving, compassionate, and wise. Send forgiveness where it is needed. Happiness is essential; it means living with unconditional love and it is the highest vibration of abundance. It comes from healthy relationships, improving bodily health, and creating freedom to step into your unique self so that you feel confident and on purpose, motivated and inspired. You are the very center of your universe. If you meet darkness, you be the Light, the Brightness. Be helpful and of service to others; make connections. In a moment of conflict, use your imagination to find a thousand solutions, because there is nothing that you cannot transcend. You need to keep looking for the possibilities and not at the problems. If you need help, do something about it. Ask for it. Your prayers are heard by thousands of beings and they will come and help you. Remember to be grateful for whatever you have. Be humble and willing to learn from the children and the animals. We want you to flourish and live in God's graciousness. Every day is a miracle day. Know that you are immortal, all-powerful, and all-loving. Thank you for being the wonderful person that you are. Thank you for your help.

You and Hathor bow to each other. The other stars gather closely around you. The light is so bright; the atmosphere is vibrating and oscillating with the highest frequency. The music of the spheres is singing in your ears. You feel overjoyed, in an ecstatic state of bliss. Just absorb all this delicious energy. You feel Hathor's messages imprinted on your soul. This is the information that you must take home to Earth now and share.

One by one, the stars come to you and gently place a hand on your heart as a blessing and a gift. You can feel the engraving of love from each one. Lastly, Hathor comes to hug you. She fills your hands with light. Then every star returns to its place in the Pleiades cluster and you feel a shower of blue light descending. You understand that it is time for you to pull all parts of yourself back together. The blue portal of light extends below you and you are called to its energy. You begin to spiral back down through time and space to Earth.

And then there you are, standing in the middle of the emerald meadow again. But it is daytime now and the sun is shining. You can clearly see your way through the forest, so you follow the path. You put your hands on your heart and feel that it is still full of light and love. This helps you to know that you have received the teachings within and now it is time to share them. As you come out of the forest, you see a family having a picnic and the children are playing and laughing. You go to greet them and wish them a wonderful day, leaving a little bit of your light with them.

River Messages

Heavy teardrops fall to earth, they gather,
Flowing together. Rivers emerge angry, raging,
Tearing away pieces of earth; clumps that matter.
Dissolving, discussing, delivering their messages
Along the course, known by stars and seers.

Boiling, thrashing, effervescing, they pass
Strong stones, swirling, sharing stories, worries.
Misty vapors seen by winds and sweet grass
Waft the secrets and seeds over the land.
Cultivating the warnings of ignorance.

Rushing down, carving away, passing buttes,
They waste their anxious cries on the desert air.
Slowing, greeting cottonwoods, the grasslands,
Sharing quiet communion with wolves and deer,
All willing to partake in the blessing, the knowing.

Broadly, passing through the cities, they watch
The busy bridges, busy buildings, busybodies.
Full of important information now, they pour
Out their hearts to each passerby, but keep on,
Out to sea where they merge with all the waters.

Dispirited, conferring, their sadness ignored,
The teardrops reconfigure to fuse with the Sun.
Light, power, energy renewed, they review
Their journey, all their work, disregarded.
They reform into drops, rivers, messages, returning.

Selva and the First Prophets

I am not sure how smart it was for me to travel during the time of the COVID pandemic from Norway all the way to the rainforests of Chiapas, Mexico. There, a massive parade of desperate immigrants, tired and hungry, passes through Central America on their northern trek toward hopeful freedom. And there, drug lords oversee their deals in a murderous manner. But gratefully what I found when I arrived was a population of lovely, smiling people, happy to be helpful. Their doggies were running free and pleased to be lying in the warm roadways, requiring us to drive around them.

Intoxicating was the rainforest with vines climbing everywhere and huge trees full of howler monkeys, beautiful birds, and jaguars stalking in the shadows. Although I never saw a jaguar, our guide had many pictures of them on his phone, even the sacred black ones. The protective jaguar energy was palpable as we walked along through the jungle.

What I did see was an ever-present verdant ocean of green, the kind that is so full of love, like the perceived color of the heart chakra. Sprinkled in this green expanse were winding, sparkling streams of pure, clear water and the brightest of tropical flowers blooming in the most unexpected places. To sit next to one of these quiet little streams of glittering water, completely surrounded by the canopy of lush green light, felt like being held in the arms of our Mother Earth. It was healing and it felt so right to be there in the forest, even during Covid.

We were there to visit the ancient Maya temples. No one knows when these temples were built. The stories passed down from Maya elders tell of beautiful statues that they have found, allegedly brought to the Yucatan from Atlantis. These oral traditions are filled with accounts of giant people who came to the Yucatan, and they are featured in many of the stelas found at the ancient sites. (A stela is an upright stone slab typically bearing a relief design.)

According to legends, the builders of the temples and pyramids were related to the Atlanteans, so these structures are possibly 12,000 years old or older. Many people agree that the survivors from Atlantis went on to help start the ancient civilizations of the Egyptians, Aztecs, Mayas, and others. Studying the architecture, geometry, astrological alignments, and symbolism in these ancient buildings, it is apparent that the builders had help from realms beyond our present-day world. It is interesting to note that even with all of our modern engineering capabilities, we would not be able to construct these buildings with the precise measurements that they showcase.

One of the temples we went to visit is called Yaxchilan. Before the 45-minute boat ride up the river, we drove through many miles of beautiful rainforests, through a tiny town, Frontera Corozal, ending up at a campsite-turned-hotel at the edge of the jungle on the Usumacinta River. Befriending us there were all the children of the village, wanting to sell us the jewelry and decorations they had learned to make using the seeds of the plants that grow in the rainforest. They were an inventive, sweet group and we did buy lots of unique and lovely things from them; it was hard to say no to their darling faces.

Following a night's sleep, the best Mexican coffee in the world and a little breakfast, we boarded our small motorboats and prepared for our ride up the river. This is a special river, filled with green water; the name Usumacinta translates to the River of Jade. It is interesting to note that in the Maya tradition, green jade represents the heart chakra. As the Usumacinta winds its way through the rainforest, it reminds me of the serpent, representing the Mother. Just imagine traveling in the belly of the green serpent to visit one of many temples built along the shores of ancient Atlantean civilizations. This was truly a journey to seek rebirth and wisdom. We arrived in a sacred manner at this ancient Atlantean city.

After the breathtaking trip, filled with sightings of crocodiles lazing along the river banks, we gingerly stepped off the boats onto a land that felt pristine and untouched. We were at a place called Yaxchilan. From Maya this translates as the City of the First Prophets. What does this mean? I came to learn that the First Prophets were the women. They were at Yaxchilan to gather visions from the fifth dimension. Their work was to decipher these messages so they could explain them in a way that would enrich the spirits of the people. It takes time to decipher the truth, so they were there in deep meditation with this work.

As we entered the site, the howler monkeys were making a huge racket, swinging from the trees above. They seemed, in a way, to be greeting us. It was so loud; it felt like a welcoming ceremony. We arrived there during the time of the total solar eclipse in early December 2021. This was projected to be an auspicious time, and I was excited about what could possibly happen at such a special place.

It was a strenuous walk up to the grand ceremonial plateau area. Arriving there, it was nearly impossible to explain the expansive feeling when first beholding that Great Plaza of Yaxchilan, but it felt wonderful. A broad, flat area with assorted ruined temples arranged around the edges of the rainforest, it extended the length of several football fields. The plaza represents a cross, the intersection of masculine and feminine, time and space, and where the Four Directions connect.

The trees growing there were so big that one could walk into their root systems, which extend up into their trunks, enabling a person to be engulfed by tree spirit energy. The huge Ceiba trees, considered to be the Trees of Life, represent three levels of the Maya cosmovision. The roots spiral nine levels deep down into Mother Earth. The trunk represents the Earth plane and the Four Directions. The leafy branches reaching so high represent the Sky, nine more levels up (As above, so below).

We learned that the priests and priestesses of ancient times meditated inside the root cavities of these vast trees for days. In all humility, they would crawl into the hollow of a tree and lie in the fetal position, praying to be reborn, while listening to the messages of Mother Earth. This practice is similar to entering a sweat lodge, which is an indigenous North American prayer ceremony. The ruler of another important Maya temple called Palenque would journey many miles to Yaxchilan, walking several days through the jungles, crossing rivers, and braving all the dangers with the intention of honoring the Mother of all nature and the divine feminine which is so evident there. It is easy to understand why Yaxchilan is considered an incredibly powerful temple site.

Our first stop was for a ceremony at the lowest level of the temple site. It featured a stela of a woman with a cord running through her tongue. I believe this means, "Be careful what you say because words have power." Wisdom (the rope, representing the serpent) needs to pass through your words for them to express truth. The tongue represents the duality that happens on our Earth because the tongue is divided down the middle into two parts. What a person says will either make things better or destroy them. We need to be careful what we say because words have power.

Our guide, Miguel Angel, is a Maya priest, taught by a lineage of ancient priests. He wanted us to accomplish at least one important thing in this vast place that day: to understand the connection between the Heart of the Earth and the Heart of the Sky.

On the middle (Earth) plane of the temple site, we encountered a stela of a priestess holding a crystal skull in her right hand. According to Miguel Angel, the priestess was showing us that we are living here in the third dimension.

A deeper teaching revealed that when we properly use the crystal skull that she offered, we can energetically rise up along the 33 vertebrae in the spine to the top of our own heads. Then we can reactivate the spiritual gifts that exist there. Along this journey, we pass through the seven chakras, creating spiritual connections all the way up.

Lars Muhl, a Danish mystic, has elaborated on the upward path of spiritual energy through the seven energy centers. Starting at the scrotum or root chakra, we are dealing with security issues, essentially how to survive. We progress to the second, sacral chakra. Here we process relationship and life force issues.

Next, we come to the solar plexus, where through our spiritual work we can find peace. On to the heart chakra, which is all about unconditional love that is filled with mercy. Then as we work our way up the spine, we arrive at the throat chakra; here we process truth. At the place of the third eye, first and foremost, we find freedom as we deal with the forgiveness of others and, most importantly, ourselves.

Finally, we arrive at the crown chakra, where we encounter the light and all the clarity that comes with it. This is where we can become One Being. The challenge is to often and consciously use the exercise of working up this ladder of inner transformation. It takes time and practice to accomplish spiritual advancement.

It is good to understand that there is a period of waiting for metamorphosis to occur, similar to the chrysalis stage of the emerging butterfly. In the stela the priestess, Mother Nature, the sacred feminine on the Earth plane, is offering you and me the gift of the crystal skull from her right hand. With it we have the opportunity to create this transformation for ourselves.

The essential piece of information about the crystal skull is that it exactly replicates our own heads. It shows us that we can and need to transform our thoughts and our minds, in order to make them clear. Consequently, we can bring ourselves into a Christ-like consciousness, full of positive energy, expanding light and love, manifesting a better world.

The Magic of the Real World

At this point in our ceremonial time at Yaxchilan, we had received the signal to ascend toward the energy of heaven, up to Temple 33 at the very top of the site, so those of us who could, purposefully climbed up many narrow, slippery stone steps to the top of the site. Once there, we were educated as to what this Temple 33 site was about.

First of all, we were introduced to a tall, massive stalactite quartz crystal standing directly in the middle of the platform and pointing straight up to the heavens.

It had been moved, presumably from a cave and up all those stone steps to the area by the ancients. None of us understood how this could have been done. We were instructed to hold the crystal with our hands and place our foreheads against it, so each in turn did this. When it was my turn, I began to weep silently, overwhelmed with emotion, because I felt such a profound love coming from deep down in the Earth.

I actually have never felt anything like it before in my life. There was a warmth in my body and it changed how my heart felt. I loved it. It became clear that the crystal had been placed there as a type of antenna to help people make the connection from deep down in the heart of our Mother Earth, through our own hearts, up to the heart of the sky. In other words, to be connected to the All.

Next, we turned our attention to the three rooms of Temple 33, located behind the crystal stalactite. The room in the middle is the most informative. There is a statue of a king-priest inside, but it has no head. Instead, the head is sitting on the floor next to it. The head has been set aside, representing a psychological modification. This is certainly a concept to ponder.

The suggested message is that to gain a new consciousness, the ego needs to be minimized to let the heart take over. It truly involves sacred work to evolve spiritually. This is what the women were doing at the City of the First Prophets. They spent time developing the spiritual messages they received in the fifth dimension so that they could teach the people what was important—that we each work hard at spiritual transformation by becoming better people, focusing on respect, love, and honor for each other and our beautiful Mother Earth.

This is truly the only way we can save our Earth.

We were given time for meditation. I laid down on some stones in between the stalactite crystal and the door of the headless deity to do my meditation. It was a comfortable, warm day, cooled by a gentle breeze and the shade of the giant trees. I felt extremely happy to be there in the presence of the First Prophets.

I closed my eyes and listened to the rainforest sounds: birds singing and the distant howler monkeys. I felt the energy of the immense trees. After a while, I saw a giant tree open its trunk, and there, standing inside the trunk, was a very tall being dressed in a pale lavender gown. It seemed like it stepped straight out of the Lord of the Rings story, with elfin ears and long blonde hair.

It was impossible to say whether it was male or female; actually, it seemed androgynous. Whatever it was, it stayed there in the frame of the tree trunk and I deeply felt the presence of this tall, beautiful being. Ethereally it befriended me.

While I experienced this silent connection, I heard the busy wings of a hummingbird whirling back and forth in the air above my chest.

I remembered teachings about the hummingbird: it represents the arrival of the new era, the new consciousness. The hummingbird equals magic medicine, because it always sees the beauty in everything. It finds every flower, it finds the love, it is connected to the heart. This is the lesson for us: to find the beauty in every person, every situation, even those we do not respect so much, because every person is a flower.

The other gift from the hummingbird is that it teaches us how to get the honey out. Honey is the most nurturing of foods and just one taste contains the energy of thousands of flowers. It is recommended that we have a little honey every day.

Selva and the First Prophets

During our current times, we need to focus on learning something from the people and the situations we encounter. We need to receive the gift that each of these opportunities offers us. The medicine from the hummingbird helps us find the beautiful flower in anybody and everybody and also to gather that honey sweetness for our own well-being.

I listened to the soft breeze in the trees above me, the leafy shadows moving in and out of my consciousness. I connected back to the being in the tree dressed in pale lavender and asked about this.

"Yes" was the answer that I heard. "This is the time for connecting with the beauty, light, and love from all around the universe and I will help you to do this. There are golden particles of light and we need to weave them together. This will help the Earth and everything on it."

I communicated back that I felt this to be true and that I wanted to participate. My friend, the beautiful being, told me that it would help me to participate in the work. The name that came into my mind on the soft breeze was "Selva." I knew immediately that this was a new guide for a new age.

I offered a great thank you that wafted up, infused with a golden light, out of my heart. Before coming back to my awakened life, I felt an imprint of energy on my etheric body and I understood that this being with whom I had been communicating was creating a deep connection with me. Back with the group, I only shared that I had connected with a new guide for this new age.

Shortly after returning home to Norway, I needed help in healing a family member. I called on Selva that night before falling asleep, envisioning the elegant being in the lavender gown. I explained the situation and asked for help. At about 3:00 a.m. I woke up and saw my guide, the Lavender Being, held in the darkness like it was still in the tree trunk. I was amazed at what happened next.

A hand reached out, offering me a symbol that I had never seen before because it seemed to be from a different language. Although it was not a hieroglyphic or a QR code, it reminded me of something just like that but more sacred. It was the vibration that I noticed. Shortly after, I fell back asleep. It all happened so fast, but I knew that I wasn't dreaming because it was as vivid in my memory as the bright sun. The next day,

Selva and the First Prophets

gratefully and almost unbelievably, the issue with my family member was resolved.

I realized that if I am truly blessed, I will be receiving help from Selva by way of codes that belong to another language, perhaps even another civilization. These come with a special vibration, like the sound of honeybees that heal. I look forward to continuing my work with this amazing being. Thank you, Selva, for being there. I accept and honor your help, wherever you come from.

Pondering Notes

The ancient Maya translation for Yaxchilan is Yax=First; Chi=Mouth; Lan=Deeply: "The one who speaks deeply." This is the energy of the spirit. A question that my guide and Maya Priest, Miguel Angel Vergara Calleros, often asks is, "Do we actually know how to use the ancient knowledge in the powerful spiritual way that it was intended?"

Maya/Atlantean Connection

Along the sacred Usumacinta River, there are at least ten ancient Maya centers. The original energies that exist there are all being held underground. They are Atlantean in nature because they are surrounded by water and also presumed to be so by the Maya priests and priestesses because of the things they have discovered at these sites.

The First Prophets Were Women

It makes sense that the First Prophets were women, because women hold an open space in their wombs to be a fertile ground for creation. As we carry children, we are receptive to unknown mysteries and are unafraid of what may come. We bravely face what is not known for the future and we are willing to change our lives to become more whole. In many older indigenous cultures, women were the most powerful, highly honored members of society. Women give birth to creation.

Heart of the Sky/ Heart of the Earth

Besides the First Prophets at Yaxchilan, there was a dynasty of four rulers known as the Bird-Jaguar Kings. This named combination of animals shows that the temple was a place to explore the relationship between the Heart of the Sky (Bird) and the Heart of the Earth (Jaguar). This is the exact relationship that our guide wanted us to better understand during our time at Yaxchilan.

We did accomplish this as we climbed from the stela with the crystal skull up to Temple 33 with the headless King-Priest. We went consciously and purposefully, experiencing the rising of the serpent up the seven energy centers and the 33 vertebrae.

Crystal Skulls

I learned a lot about the crystal skull from Miguel Angel. There is nothing written in historical texts about crystal skulls, so I did not know anything about them before visiting the Maya temples. I learned that they exist throughout the Maya lands and also in South Africa, Greece, Albania, Egypt, Tibet, and most probably China. Some believe they were brought by the gods who wanted to develop the human race to have a more advanced consciousness.

There is a place in the Maya lands where the crystal skulls are particularly cherished. Buried deep in Tres Zapotes, the Maya Elders know where these ancient skulls are hidden. They are keeping them safe there, because they believe the skulls maintain the energetic balance of the axis of the planet and keep the vibration of the planet in harmony.

Furthermore, the Elders believe that a total of 520 crystal skulls were originally brought to planet Earth by different interstellar races. They were influenced by various constellations, among them the Pleiades, Orion, and Andromeda. Most probably they were delivered during Lemurian times, 100,000 years ago, by the cosmic gardeners, otherwise known as the winged ones, angels, and archangels.

The original ancient crystal skulls are made of the clearest quartz crystal. Notably, the main quality of quartz is to store information. Spiritually, crystals can only conduct highly refined energy and this is their power. Part of the beauty of our Mother Earth is that it is filled with crystals everywhere. In our galaxy there are crystal planets; it is a highly beneficial exercise to connect with them.

When we look into one of these original crystal skulls, we will see a diagram of the universe, filled with planets and star systems. We can also see by way of an actual map that the third eye is connected to the pineal gland. It has been shown that when an original crystal skull is lit up, holograms are revealed whereby we can see symbols of the Sun, special constellations and sacred areas like the observatory at Chichen Itza or the Potala of Tibet. These skulls can transport us into other dimensions and otherworldly places like belts of asteroids. In El Mirador, an archaeological site in Guatemala, there are 5,000 temples that are yet to be unveiled. There, the Maya Elders are guarding the most critical crystal skulls.

Devas and Androgyny

Selva, my beautiful guide in the tree, is most probably a deva of this amazing rainforest, witnessing through many thousands of years the beauty of nature and the power of the divine feminine. The main purpose of a deva is to keep harmony with Mother Nature, a most important role in our world today and especially at Yaxchilan.

Selva is an androgynous being, one who is a blurring of the difference between men and women. Our sacred dolphins live this way. Androgynous beings are beyond masculine and feminine, yet they are able to use whatever male powers and female powers they need. This is a growing phenomenon in our world today. It is said that in Lemurian times, this was how everyone existed. Maybe it is a foreshadowing of our future days. Some current spiritual leaders have had visions of androgynous babies coming forth. Perhaps this represents our new humanity.

Sacred Geometry

The symbol that I received from Selva when I woke up in the middle of the night was certainly mathematical and filled with sacred geometry, providing a particular healing resonance for the situation of my relative. This kind of frequency can come to us through devas, angels, and other special beings from the original levels of creation. The sound of buzzing bees is indicative of the etheric plane. I was deeply grateful, albeit surprised, and I am looking forward to more communication of this kind.

Eclipses

Eclipses are famous for delivering events, opportunities, information, meetings, and relationships that carry our lives in a completely new direction. Some of the information that I gathered about this particular solar eclipse on December 4, 2021, is that it would be the start of a new 19-year cycle and an initiation into a new level of consciousness. Information from various students of astrology elaborated further that there would be a cleansing of old belief systems that would yield a new paradigm.

This paradigm would support truth, freedom, higher consciousness, and wisdom. This is the result of a massive download of energy as the Earth moves through the photon belt and surges of light plasma enter our cells. This is actually more than just light; it carries with it divine intelligence. We can indeed see the bright light. It is all around.

The golden particles that Selva and I discussed are being seen by many people on our Earth at this time. We ourselves are actually particles of light. There seems to be a healing web of light forming around our planet. As we hold this light within us, we can connect with other lightworkers and support each other in attunement to our Earth.

The particular eclipse of 2021 was projected to be full of fantastic dreams leading us to our own higher guidance. It certainly was an accurate prediction for me and my time at Yaxchilan.

Meditation with the Tree of Life

To access a video recording of the meditation, scan this code:

    This meditation is about the Tree of Life. The Tree of Life is an archetypal image found in popular culture and also in most of the world's mythological, philosophical, and religious traditions. Trees have roots that grow deep into the soil of our earth's creation and they have branches that reach up toward the heavens. Therefore, they represent a force that connects all of life.

    Besides showing a connection between all living things, the Tree of Life can represent a path to enlightenment, a connection between the physical and spiritual aspects of the universe and the cycle of life and death.

    We will start our meditation by going to a special sacred garden. Notice your surroundings as you approach this magical place. The garden is sweet and beautiful, the ground is covered with soft green grass and flowers that bloom along its edges. In the distance, you can see tall, strong trees.

    Before entering into this sacred garden, you take off your shoes so that you can feel a greater connection with Mother Earth and all of her special mystical presence. Now in your bare feet, you step into the garden. As you move, you can feel the soft grass on the soles of your feet. When you look around, you see flower blossoms in all their brilliant colors. It seems like there is a bit of heaven in each one. You feel a magical attraction here. You can smell the honeysuckle, lavender, and the roses. Above in the blue sky, you hear birds singing. They seem happy.

You listen as the breeze whispers through the branches of the trees. Looking up, you see how high the trees have grown. These trees have been growing here for a very long time. You are drawn to walk further on into the forest. There is something familiar about it. It feels safe, comfortable, and fresh here. There is an otherworldly feel in this part of the forest. You begin to notice that there are elemental light beings, orbs of light, playing all around you. You walk over to a huge oak tree, the one with the biggest trunk. This oak tree is so big that when you put your arms around it to give it a hug, your hands cannot reach all the way around but you know that the tree feels your love.

As you stand next to this tree, you can feel its strength. You can see how its thick roots grow from the trunk down into the soil of creation. Gazing up, you see the sunlight filtering down through the leaves. This is the tree you have chosen to be with in order to commune with the energies of the Tree of Life.

Take a deep breath in through your nose, smelling the perfume of the garden. The scent of the lavender flowers fills your soul with relaxing happiness. With a deep sigh let your breath out through your mouth. Take a few more deep breaths like this. With each breath your shoulders drop and you become more relaxed. As you stand there next to the tree, the tree invites you inside its big trunk. It simply opens up a space for you to step inside… so you do. This Tree of Life has understood that you are open to learning from its great wisdom. Now you are inside of the tree.

You look around and everything is green. This is soothing for your eyes. A loveliness arises from this color green. You relax more as any anxiety that you may have felt from stepping inside the tree is soothed away. You feel the peace of the green energy; it helps you to feel comfortable and hopeful that perhaps you will understand something from the great Tree of Life. You begin to notice how easy it is to breathe inside the tree. Take a deep, delicious breath through your nose and slowly exhale through your mouth. You remember now that the trees provide pure oxygen for humans. They literally give us human beings the oxygen that sustains our essential life! When we breathe out, they receive their nourishment from us. It is an amazing cycle of life. Take some deep breaths as you feel gratitude for the healing power of the trees.

Still standing inside the tree, you reach your hands out, touching the inside of the trunk. It feels strong and you feel secure. You remember seeing the thick roots going down into the Earth and you realize how stable and strong the tree is. The roots grow down through the dirt to the spring waters of the Earth. This is where the tree gets the nourishment to grow. You open your heart to the feelings that run deep into Mother Earth and realize that you are like this tree because you, too, are rooted in the Earth and you, too, receive your nutrients from the soul of creation, Mother Earth. All your food and fresh water come from her. Your spiritual connection with the plants and animals comes through your roots in the Earth. Give your great thanks to Mother Earth now. All of this helps you to understand that you yourself are strong and grounded like the tree.

From inside the tree, you can feel above you a rustling of the leaves and the branches moving with the wind. As you look up, you can see that above you, the tree is indeed moving. The branches seem flexible, they move without breaking in the wind. You realize that you can also be flexible, that you can change, you can adjust and you can heal without breaking.

The small leaves ripple in the breeze. The light coming through them beckons you to venture out and connect with the warm face of Father Sun, so you stretch up and out into the top of the tree into the leafy branches. Understanding that Father Sun provides light and warmth and life-giving forces for the tree and for you, you give thanks to Father Sun for all his blessings.

Beyond Father Sun, you can further see that there is a wide, beautiful sky full of stars, moons, planets, and galaxies. These are the star tribes of our planet. With great wonder, you understand that we receive the starlight and the moonlight that they send down to us on Earth with love, even when we can't see it. Looking beyond the upper branches of the big oak tree, you reach up high with your hands to catch some of that love that is falling down to our Earth at this time. You hear a message in the whispering wind.

The message for you is to decide what you think Mother Earth needs now more than anything else. The reason the star tribes want this information is so that they can send help to our lives here by expanding our love. Whatever you think is needed on Earth now is what you need to focus on. It can be something wonderful.

Take your time to think about this. When you have your answer, you instantly receive in your raised hands a golden ball of Light. The heavens have gifted you some special extra Light for planet Earth. This Light will allow your prayer to manifest the help that you wish for our Earth. You take this ball of golden light, this gift from the heavens, and gently place it on the ground here inside the tree on Mother Earth.

You touch the inside trunk of the tree. The beautiful spirit of the Tree of Life opens up and you look out at the light of day where the warm sun is shining in the sacred garden. You thank the beautiful Tree of Life for all you have understood from it and you step out. It has been quite a journey, so you sit down next to the lavender flowers to slowly contemplate what you have learned.

All the green energy from inside the tree has given you a feeling of rebirth. Reviewing your time there, you realize that the Tree of Life is your Mother and your Father. Also, you realize that you have received a new sense of balance. This comes from the experience that you are both strong and grounded yet flexible and able to adapt to pressures without breaking apart.

You lie down on the soft grass, stretching out. The sun shines on your face and a butterfly dances in front of your eyes. After enjoying this dance for a while, you slowly realize that it may be time to leave the sacred garden. When you are ready, slowly get up and walk past the heavenly flowers out to where your shoes are waiting for you.

Super Full Moon

I watched in the east until the giant yellow Moon showed up through the leafy branches of the trees. It was as big and full as they said it would be. Quite overwhelmed with its energy, I stood quietly for a while, bathed in its golden light.

With the warm summer air all around, I slowly took off my clothes and danced—naked, graceful and free in the energy of this beautiful moonlight, offering myself up to it in total trust. A gentle breeze caressed my body like the kisses of a lover. The perfumed night air consumed my soul as I succumbed to the delightful bliss of the goddess Moon.

Cicadas harmonized the sounds from the darkness like a perfectly pitched crystal bowl. Thank you, Moon, for all this love. I silently offered the thanksgiving prayer.

I felt the golden circle of cosmic Moon energy radiating down to Earth with messages for our next turn. There was an opalescent light shining out in double rainbow rings from our Moon. Already it had set the ocean's patterns, the tides within our bodies, and the beauty of the night skies. Now we can work with the Moon's energy directly and even more synergistically.

Thank you, powerful, beautiful, wonderful Moon. We will remember your full circle of time, circle of love, and circle of life.

Pondering Notes

The Moon is a beautiful, sacred feminine being that everyone can easily see and feel. The blessings of our Mother Moon are extraordinarily accessible and we can all acknowledge them. As her light shines down on us, she makes each one of us feel like we are her special one. This particular Super Full Moon left me infatuated with her love and blessings.

We know our Mother Moon around the world by different names and they all have feminine characteristics. This is because of her divine feminine energy. In Spanish, she is known as Luna, in Sanskrit as Chandra, Gaelic as Ghealach, Incan as Killa, Lakota as Hanhepi Wi.

There are many different monthly names for our Moon depending on the environment and culture. Most indigenous cultures have a different name for each moon of the lunar year because of the way she helps determine the weather, the migration of animals, and navigation. For example, in January, the name of the moon could be translated to Wolf Moon; in February, Snow Moon; next, Worm Moon, Pink Moon, Flower Moon, Strawberry Moon, Buck Moon, Sturgeon Moon, Corn Moon, Hunter's Moon, Beaver Moon and Cold Moon.

In many of the ancient indigenous cultures there were thirteen moons in a year. Indigenous peoples of the Earth know and respect the wisdom and power of the turtle. Held within a turtle's shell is the knowledge of time and the wisdom of the thirteen moons, indicating the power of cosmic knowledge.

> *"To remember that Earth is Turtle Island is to remember the way of the Earth as it is guided by the cosmic power of thirteen moons."*
> **—Indigenous Grandmother**

Thirteen scales make up the back of the turtle's shell. It takes thirteen moons for Earth to go around the Sun just one time. Among the indigenous peoples of North America, Earth is known as Turtle Island.

Super Full Moon

In the original time the turtle's wisdom was known by every child of the Earth. Children knew that the path of thirteen moons was the one to walk. It was a path of life that needed no explaining. Now with the Gregorian calendar adopted throughout most of the world, there are only twelve months in a calendar year but still thirteen full moons. Perhaps this is why life can seem confusing.

Our Moon provides gentle help for our bodies by keeping everything in balance, both inside and outside. Balance supports the capacity of an entity to self-regulate and adapt to challenges in the environment. The Moon rules the waters of the world, including the tides and the water within our bodies. Since we are composed mostly of water, this impacts our emotions, intuition, and psyche.

Moon ceremonies are important because they help us to stay synchronized with our Earth and ourselves. The New Moon is a powerful time to reset goals, to pray for what we need for ourselves, our family, our community, and the Earth. It is also a time to move toward healing, happiness, and prosperity in all aspects of life. The Full Moon signals a time for reflection. This is when we can appreciate that the seeds we planted earlier are starting to blossom in the light. It is a time for thanksgiving.

There are in fact nine separate phases of the moon. Trudy Woodcock of Casa K'in in Yucatan, Mexico, channels Lady Zak-Kuuk, a Maya Priestess of the Light. This is what Lady Zek-Kuuk says about the phases of the moon:

"With each cycle of the Moon, you move into the unknown. With each phase of the moon, you gather the insight needed to manifest who you truly are and what is being asked of you at this time. With the completion of each Moon cycle, you expand your consciousness and step up to another level, where you create what you truly want in your life now."

She outlines the phases as follows:

New Moon: This phase creates from the darkness, all good things; like the womb, it gives birth to a cycle of creativity and possibility.

Waxing Crescent Moon: A time to determine what you want to create and how it will impact you personally.

First Quarter Moon: The opportunity to notice how your creation will benefit others in the community and around the world.

Super Full Moon

Waxing Gibbous Moon: A time full of anticipation and wonder to gather support for whatever it is you want.

Full Moon: This is an open door in the night sky, inviting you to enter the mysteries and feel the healing touch of the goddess. At this time, the moon acts as a mirror, reflecting the truth without any doubts.

Waning Gibbous Moon: Wake-up call to stop dreaming and see the reality of what you are working on.

Waning Three-Quarter Moon: An outward expression of your inner awakening. A time to clean out and put things in order for the outward expression of your intention.

Waning Crescent Moon: When you gain assurance of how the manifestation will occur, following the three laws of manifestation. These illustrate how your creation will benefit you, secondly the community and third, the Earth.

Dark Moon: Here the light moves inside of you, where inner transformation is taking place. Now the moon steps out of the night sky into your heart and the third eye opens. This initiates the next level of the upward spiral.

These phases of the moon move quickly. Following them helps us to remain conscious and on track for becoming contributing members of society and being happier people.

Unlike the Sun, the Moon is always with us, night and day like a caring and supportive mother, so it is both essential and wonderful to acknowledge her for her amazing gift of motherly comfort and love.

Albert Einstein once said, "The most beautiful emotion we can experience is the mystical. It is the source of all true art and science." It is essential to remember that mysticism is about personal experience. No one can encounter it for anybody else; one participates in it for one's own self-development. Some things happen only once, and really, there is no way that we can predict when magic will happen. We need to put ourselves out there in Nature, open our eyes, and feel blessed when we receive special gifts from the spirit world.

Super Full Moon

CONCLUSION

I provided seven of my own personal, mystical, shamanic stories, but there are many more stories from many others. I share these with you, hoping that you can see how easy it is and, more importantly, how awesome it is to travel into other dimensions of space and time.

I have been stunned by the creativity of our universe. It is wise to experiment with this mystical work now, because it is the right time to do so. We each have an important personal responsibility to advance our own spirituality during these challenging times.

In this era, we can all access the fifth dimension by traveling to other universes and realities and dreaming our way into these places. We can fly through portals with no limitations. Portals are life-changing, shifting processes. In these stories, there are many portals that are passed through. The dream visions described happened on sacred mountains, near special waters or other potent areas of our Earth, because the portals are actually powerful beings in and of themselves. When we ask for help, they will guide us through time and space to other realities and dimensions. They are witnesses to our evolution and can tell us stories of cosmic gardeners, connecting to an ancestry that transcends time. We can also use their help to travel anywhere and to assist others in need.

This interdimensional traveling is an emerging energetic experience, yielding an increased capacity for self-mastery. Here, our souls—not egos—are in charge of our journeys. Why is this helpful? Because these realizations will encourage us to let go of outdated programs and material preoccupations and allow for their transmutation into higher forms of awareness.

With a more informed level of consciousness, intelligence, and experience, we can expand our reality and better understand the vastness of our lives and spirits.

The most important part of all this exploration is to find ways to learn and heal from the experiences that we encounter. I have spent a lot of time pondering being embraced by the Light of the Living Universe and the magic of our world. Integrating all this into my life is an ongoing process. If you choose to experiment with this type of spiritual, mystical activity, I have some advice.

First, be sure to record your experience as soon as you can. Write about it or create a picture to keep it vivid in your imagination. Connect with spiritual teachers from different lineages because they can help you understand the experiences from different points of view. It is most important to serve others, even by simply saying to a stranger, "Have a beautiful day!" Love and joy create coherent, positive, and happy energies. Serving others will help you stay happy.

When you make your world more harmonious, it will encourage the development of a higher consciousness. As you work on becoming a better person, it will help you to integrate the mystical experiences you have encountered. You will gain more insight and end up trusting more in life.

The teachers I am listening to at this time from around the globe are saying that our number one job on Earth right now is to be happy. Why is this? It is necessary to understand that if you are looking for happiness, you will not find it out there somewhere. Happiness does not exist outside of yourself; you can only find it within. Therefore, you need to develop spiritually so that you can cultivate the element of happiness within.

Happiness exists right now for everyone, with no prerequisites. It is a state of mind directly linked to your own awareness. Journeying into other realms is a joyous, fun experience, a doorway into other potentialities that, importantly, offers you a bright future.

The integration work is the most important part of shamanism. In my story from Yaxchilan, the First Prophets spent time in meditation to understand the messages that they received, intended to be delivered to their people. I have similarly provided interpretations for you from my visions for these times that we are now in. They are in the Pondering Notes after each story.

We are all currently in a transformative process. During the steps of becoming a butterfly, there is a time when the caterpillar morphs into a chrysalis. This is a period of simply not knowing what will happen yet with a belief that the good beauty will come forth. This is where we are now in our current world situation. It takes time to interpret the truth. It is important to believe that with time, the beautiful new butterfly will emerge.

Find a community to be a part of, one that calls to you, because it is easier to be strong together with others. Different groups of people say that there is a healing web of energy and light forming around our planet. As we hold this light within us, we can connect with other lightworkers and support each other. Let us use, as Dante says, "the love that moves the Sun and the other stars" to move ourselves forward.

The headless priest at the top of the pyramid in Yaxchilan, from the story "Selva and the First Prophets," exhibits exactly what our task is. Instead of working from the head and the ego, it is time to work more directly from the heart. We may be filled with the shadow of our traumas and dramas, which are constantly trying to distract us. However, what we need to focus on is the endless mercy radiating from the diamond transcendence, which is always pouring towards us, filling us with hope and faith. (See the many instances in the book, especially in the "Mt. Shasta" and "Dolphin Journey" stories.)

Remember that no matter what we have done, as expressed in the "Dolphin Journey" story, grace is always available to heal and transfigure us. This is the time to give all that we can from our heart centers. It is time to be happy with whatever comes our way because everything is happening for an important reason. There is a harmony in the spheres and it is time for us to get back in tune with that. We can think about becoming Homoluminous Ones.

Our population is riding a spiritual wave of evolution. Coming through many teachers at this time is the concept that our entire human species is actually one single being that we each as individuals contribute to. This entire single species is developing as one organism and coming gradually together for a threshold event. When we humans become a planet of awakened souls, we will live differently. This was keenly illustrated to me in the story of "What is Abu Ghurab?", with the vision near the Pleiades when all the people were looking at the one light that was reflecting in their eyes.

In the future, humans will be connecting with divine intelligence and dissolving into Oneness. It is valuable to recognize that we are reflections of an amazing, conscious, evolutionary thought that we call our Universe. It has meaning and purpose and we need to stand for the truth and love of that. We have unlimited potential for our lives. Once we realize this, we can be less fearful of change and feel more empowered to evolve.

It is vitally important to note that even though at this time we can access the fifth dimension, we still actually live and function in the third dimension on this planet. We are not going anywhere; we are becoming more right here, so please remember that as we go traveling in this way, we must get ourselves back home or have someone help us with that. This third dimension here on Earth is where we must be most of the time in order to help others, such as our family, community, and global friends on all of our paths forward. We need to abide by the Golden Rule and treat each other the way we would like to be treated. Our service, love, guidance, and life energy are needed here.

This fact emphasizes the second important part of our responsibility in order to advance our world. The first part, as this book represents, is our own spiritual development. But the second part is just as important. It entails work within our societies to be active in bettering our real-life situations with social activism. What can we each do today to make our world better? My friend and mentor, Andrew Harvey, has a list of suggested activities (in the following condensed excerpt) from his great book, *The Hope: A Guide to Sacred Activism*.[2]

---

2 Used by permission of the author.

Conclusion

Let me offer you ten things you can do right now, or within the next twenty-four hours, to start to align yourself with the power and hope of Sacred Activism. The first six will invite you into deep, nourishing, connection with your spirit; the last four will help you express the compassion and joy this connection awakens in you in action.

Write down now one thing that today has made you feel grateful to be alive. It could be something as simple as the taste of the bagel you had for breakfast. Set aside a small notebook and make the commitment to write down one thing every day that has lit you up with joy. At the end of a month sit down and read the list out loud, slowly, to yourself. You will discover that it will remind you how blessed you are already just by being alive in a world full of ordinary wonders. You will discover, too, that it will awaken in you a passion for life and a hunger to protect and preserve it.

Now write down, without thinking too much or editing yourself, just "off the top of your heart," ten things you would say are "sacred" to you. Today my list is: friendship, all you who are reading this, justice, cats, the first roses of summer, all religions, wise elders everywhere who share their wisdom tenderly and tactfully, India, my brave and wild mother. What is your list? By writing it down you will start to be inspired by your deepest values, beliefs, and sources of emboldening joy.

Think of someone who has hurt you or betrayed you and make a commitment to work on forgiving them. Imagine them now, in front of you, surrounded by light, happy and well, and pray for them to realize their life's purpose. Just to do this once with humble sincerity will unveil in you your innate strength of compassion. You taste its truth and freedom and the desire that is born from it to see all beings happy.

Read a short text from any of the world's spiritual traditions that inspires you with the love-wisdom of those prophets and mystics who know God directly.

When the text you have chosen starts to light up your spirit, pray a short prayer that aligns you with the "pure deep love" that is longing to use you as its instrument in the world. Here are some, from different traditions, that I use at odd moments throughout my day:

- *Lord, let me live to be truly useful.*
- *Beloved, make me strong enough to do your will.*
- *Divine Mother, fill me with your passion of compassion, so I can do your work tirelessly.*

If none of these inspire you or reflect your beliefs, make up your own spontaneously and say it ten times with passion, in the core of your heart.

Make now a real commitment to spiritual practice. If you do not yet have one, start now, simply. Just sit with your back straight and watch your thoughts for three minutes and allow your mind, however briefly, to fall silent. In that silence is your greatest treasure, one that will unfold its gold in you if you commit to twenty minutes of simple sitting in the morning and evening before you go to bed. Don't believe me; try it.

Strengthened by prayer, practice, and inspiration, turn now to your life and the people in it. Everyone, especially in a time like ours, has friends who are in grief, or ill, or looking for a job or are in real financial difficulty. Commit now to ringing one of them up, and ask him or her what you could do to make their burden easier. Do this soon and be happy that you can.

Make a commitment to miss one meal in the coming twenty-four hours and send a check for the money you would have spent on it to a reputable organization dealing with world hunger. Never forget that almost two billion people live on less than a dollar a day.

The worldwide financial crisis we are now in is plunging people everywhere into financial distress. There are families in your immediate vicinity who are suffering. Make a commitment to find out who they are and what they might need. Ring six of your friends to make a commitment with you to begin supplying them with what they require. In acting like this, you will be helping to activate the kind heart of your community. In my experience, more people than you may imagine are longing to be of help; take the first step now yourself, and be surprised and heartened.

Make a commitment today, even if you are in financial difficulties, to tithe between five and ten percent of what you earn to a cause of your choice. I recommend choosing one particular cause that deeply moves you and sticking to your commitment, whatever happens; over time, tithing like this will give you a great and healing sense of being of use, and the cause you are helping will become more and more precious and personal to you, and you will want, naturally and simply, to do more.

Andrew Harvey, Founder and Director of the Institute for Sacred Activism, has walked Christian, Hindu, Buddhist, and Sufi mystical paths and has engaged in deep study in Asia and Europe with accomplished spiritual teachers. He taught at Oxford University, Cornell University, the California Institute of Integral Studies, and institutes all over the world.

He is the author of more than 30 books, including *The Hope: A Guide to Sacred Activism; Radical Passion: Sacred Love and Wisdom in Action;* and *A Journey in Ladakh.* He also co-edited Sogyal Rinpoche's *The Tibetan Book of Living and Dying.* His most recent books are *Love is Everything* and (with Carolyn Baker) *Radical Regeneration: Sacred Activism and the Renewal of the World.*

During our time on Earth, filled with alarming climate changes, war and a breakdown of economic and societal equality, we could be on the brink of extinction. However, as Jean Houston points out, it is a time reminiscent of the Black Plague of the mid-thirteenth century, when half the population of Europe died. That catastrophe birthed the great new age of the Renaissance. With the fantastic imaginations of Leonardo da Vinci, Copernicus, Galileo, Michelangelo and others came a whole new perspective of who we are in the universe. This amazing explosion of creativity created an evolution of human possibilities.

We are now in similar times. Humanity can dream a better dream than we have done in the past. Just look at all of our unsustainable systems. We need to redesign ourselves and create a world that works for everyone. We are the people to recreate a revolution in society, economics, science, the arts and consciousness. This truly is our work.

As Anneloes Smitsman of EarthWise Centre points out, "We are cosmic beings and with our cosmic genes, we have the ability, capacity, and soulfulness to become partners with the cosmic power for this time, co-creating new ideas and breakthrough events. We are living in one of the great times of a whole system transition which involves everybody. We are evolving together with nature, rising to take individual and collective responsibility. We could consider this the Newness time."

As the Hopi remind us, "We are the Ones we have been waiting for." Be brave. We are made for this—the most important time in human history.

Finally, it is important to stay connected to a spiritual role model. One that I adore is St. Francis. This saint found the Divine in all things and never banished anyone or anything from his heart.

The Prayer of St. Francis

Lord, make me an instrument of thy peace:

Where there is hatred, let me sow love;

Where there is injury, pardon;

Where there is doubt, faith;

Where there is despair, hope;

Where there is darkness, light;

Where there is sadness, joy.

Oh, Divine Master, grant that I may not so much seek to be consoled as to console;

To be understood, as to understand;

To be loved, as to love.

For it is in giving that we receive.

It is in pardoning that we are pardoned.

And it is in dying that we are born to Eternal Life.

St. Francis is the patron saint of the Environment. His Saint Day is October 4.

The reason St. Francis is so special to me is because he earned his position as a saint. He started out his life as a spoiled rascal and drunkard from an aristocratic family. Looking for fame as an army hero, he ended up in jail where he had the opportunity to think about his purpose. When he emerged, he assumed a new position of being a protector, embodying a higher purpose.

He loved and cared for the lepers; he spent time in the forests and befriended all the birds and animals, even protecting the small insects. He took care of the environment and the desperate people. He brought more Heaven to Earth by showing everyone about mercy, healing, courage, clarity, and love. He achieved a level of dedication to these virtues that truly highlighted his being as a saintly person. He is a self-made soul who can be called upon for inspiration.

Despite his rough start in life, he grew to understand his inner divinity. His loving spirit entered into the lowliest, most repulsive and most sinful of beings. It was a love of man for man and beasts. He truly learned to practice the Golden Rule. That is why I pray with him. Furthermore, one of my beloved spiritual guides is Kuthumi. It is said that in a prior incarnation he was St. Francis. I feel especially close to him.

Thank you for joining me on these adventures. My deepest wish is that we each find whichever path is most suitable to develop our souls to be as loving as possible and that we truly consider treating others as we would like to be treated. From that perspective, it is easy to engage in the social activism that is suggested here in the conclusion. We are being supported by the Universe to make significant changes at this time. Together we can improve the conditions on Earth for people, animals and all existence. It is truly a simple matter of making the decision to move in this direction.

Blessings to All.

Acknowledgments

I want to remember and thank the kind and powerful Lakota people who initiated me into their amazing spiritual world over several decades, especially Irma Bear Stops. They all taught me about the capacity that we each have to connect with the unlimited power of the universe and to realize the wonderful potential for miracles. Their Lakota spirituality is full of faith in the mercy and goodness of the Creator. It is also overflowing with gratefulness for everything that exists in creation.

Also, thank you to my wonderful and extraordinary children, who heard my prayers and came to help make my life a miraculous reality.

Great appreciation to my brilliant mentor Andrew Harvey who supported me and guided me to write this book. He convinced me that it was important for me to share my history of living a life touched by amazing teachers and by magic.

Thank you further to my dear friend, Lee Cook-Mitchell, who offered wisdom and clarity about aspects of the writing while encouraging me forward.

Credit also to some amazing young adults in Vietnam and Indonesia for the beautiful illustrations. I was happy to support them as they created these images for me.

Deepest thanks as well to Michael Henry Dunn, who helped me create the wonderful audio and videos used with the meditations. It was such a privilege to work with this award-winning Julliard-trained performer, actor and composer of devotional music.

Finally, thank you to my beautiful water angel friend, Jenny D'Angelo, who helped me with her invaluable editing process and to Ellen Gunter who gave the manuscript one last look, polishing and double-checking the details.

ABOUT THE AUTHOR
Kristina Wood

For more than 30 years, I've worked closely with the indigenous people on their sacred lands in South Dakota, learning about their ancient ways and participating with them in ceremonies. I am so grateful to have received many sacred gifts from my friends. I had profound and enlightening experiences with these beautiful people. Our relationship deepened my respect for indigenous wisdom and spirituality. I began to travel to other sacred places worldwide—Egypt, Bhutan, Peru, Ireland, and beyond. I founded and ran a travel company, Adventurous Spirit Travel, leading others on pilgrimages to connect with nature and ancient indigenous wisdom.

Inspired by all my mystical experiences while traveling, I began writing my first book: *Why the Sunflower Smiles*. My second book, *The Magic of the Real World* is now available. Both books explore how connecting with the natural world, the cosmos, and unseen dimensions of nature spirits and light beings can positively impact and heal our lives.

Now, in my mid-70s, I embrace my role as an Elder, ready to share what I've learned throughout my years, with others. I have started a new company called Mystical Nature Journeys with programs to encourage my fellow humans to seek out the sacred in everyday life.

I believe we can all partner with Nature and gain more fulfillment and self-regenerating joy in life. If you are ready to reconnect with your inner wisdom and embrace your unique journey, I offer stories, meditations, videos, courses, and sacred pilgrimages to help guide you.

These offerings are especially helpful for those who are feeling trapped in their virtual reality, or stuck in a concrete city, and are stressed, lonely, disconnected, or feeling numb. I want you to know that it is possible to find a way to feel more alive, more joy, gratitude, love and to enjoy the wonders of our amazing universe. I would like to guide you along this path.

Today, I live in Norway, where some of the happiest people in the world live along the fjords, in the mountains and on the coastlines. It is a beautiful life with my wonderful husband.

Learn more: www.mysticalnaturejourneys.com

VISIT US AT
www.floweroflifepress.com

www.ingramcontent.com/pod-product-compliance
Lightning Source LLC
Chambersburg PA
CBHW071420160426

43195CB00013B/1753